WHERE ARE THE DEAD? CAN THEY SPEAK?

Ralphael Gasson gives startling witness to the messages, voices and apparitions which he himself raised in seances. But while affirming that Spiritualists are sincere and the phenomena they call forth are real, he questions that the spirits are those of deceased human beings.

Using arguments based upon intimate, personal knowledge, and on numerous passages in the Bible, he concludes that there is deception being practiced—but deception that is not of human origin. With clarity and unique insight, he shows the subtle and profound trap into which so many well-meaning people have been lured.

THE
CHALLENGING
COUNTERFEIT

THE CHALLENGING COUNTERFEIT

Raphael Gasson

LOGOS INTERNATIONAL
PLAINFIELD, NEW JERSEY

First Printing 1966
Sixteenth Printing 1979

CONTENTS

Chapter

THE
CHALLENGING
COUNTERFEIT

CHAPTER I

FROM SATAN TO CHRIST

"All we like sheep have gone astray; we have turned every one to his own way; and the Lord hath laid on him the iniquity of us all."

ISAIAH 53, 6.

"And He hath put a new song in my mouth, even praise unto our God."

PSALM 40, 3.

BEFORE attempting to take the reader through this study of Spiritualism and the outcome of Satan's methods of deception in this field of his work, it may be to the point to offer a little proof that it is written with a certain amount of authority, since I have been actively engaged in the propagation of what, at one time, I thought to be the truth, but which eventually proved to be nothing less than demonic.

The journey, for me, from Satan to Christ, was a long and weary one, taking dangerous pathways, bringing many bitter experiences and battles against principalities and power, almost costing my life, before I reached that place called Calvary—where the Lord Jesus Christ met my need as a sinner as I surrendered my life to Him. In my travels through supernatural experiences, I was faced with the same problem that confronts thousand of others — that of trying to

11

reconcile conflicting facts and theories. It is a common weakness that when concrete facts do not match up with our preconceived theories, we prefer to keep our theories and live in an imaginary world, rather than face the facts and alter our theories to suit them. Many lengths are gone to, to preserve our theories, especially in the spiritual realm—but there comes a time when we all have to realize that fact is fact and theory is only theory and must be dealt with accordingly.

The only sensible thing for a man to do when he reaches this stage is to alter his theories to suit the facts, since the latter are of an immutable nature. For this reason, I am attempting to bring personal experiences before the Church of Christ and possibly some who are not redeemed by the precious blood of Jesus (or have not yet yielded to Him utter control of their lives), with the earnest desire that when the facts of Spiritualism are more widely known, it will be revealed what an insidious danger it contains, both for the children of God and those unenlightened people who are still outside of the Kingdom. The following pages contain not the result of speculative theories, but actual participations. It is to be admitted that when a person can talk from experience and say "this really happened to me" mental adverse arguments avail nothing.

A psychologist would no doubt attempt an explanation of changes of opinions and habits, a scientist would give a different version by pointing to various physiological changes possibly due to atmospheric conditions, while the layman would think of every conceivable reason rather than believe the testimony of the one who experienced the change. The scientist who is able to describe, with such accuracy, every minute detail of the atom bomb is still unable to produce a new creature in Christ, and with all his knowledge, is unable to change the heart of man which is desperately wicked. Only the Lord Himself is able to effect this change and in spite of all the explanations that may come from the wise and learned, we who have the experience of being born again, will leave the wise to wrangle, keeping our own counsel, because we *know* that something has happened — and we know Who has made it happen!

Facts are not always palatable, are sometimes very uncomfortable, and I trust that the ones presented here will cause the reader to seek the things of God more desperately. Once we can come to the place where we can face facts we will have to realize our utter dependence upon God, Who is indeed a reality. I went this way, and had to admit—like many others—that the only safe and secure way to live a full life was to surrender it to Christ, confessing to Him that I was a sinner and then allowing Him to run my life for me. I can now stand amazed at the greatness and tender mercies of my Lord in dying for me; by His precious blood redeeming me, and by His Spirit enabling me to live an overcoming life.

In the first chapter, I should like to bear witness as to how I sought to find salvation my own way and like a sheep, went astray, but by God's grace, eventually found it—and He found me and put a new song, not only in my mouth, but also in my heart, even praises unto my God.

I was born into a Jewish family, just after my mother's sister had died and according to Jewish tradition, was named, as near as possible, after this aunt, whose name was Rachel (intimately abbreviated to Ray). This naming procedure would have happened in any case and the subsequent strange happenings were not really needed to force the issue.

After the death of Ray, my grandparents, although orthodox Jews, began to take an interest in Spiritualism and frequented meetings in the hopes of being able to make contact with the spirit of Ray. My grandmother became a confirmed Spiritualist and although my grandfather never discussed the subject much, he apparently took some kind of interest in the Movement. This attitude was maintained until both were killed while crossing a road together in 1946.

As a result of my grandmother attending these meetings, she made several contacts with what was supposed to be the spirit of Ray and it was while Ray was presumably manifesting herself that she insisted that when I was born, I should have her name. She also appeared to my mother, making her promise that I would be named after her. Many strange things arose out of these "spirit" messages that eventually revolutionized my whole life — although it was many years before I was told of them.

True to promise and Jewish tradition, I was named Raphael—the nearest masculine equivalent—and brought up as a Jew. In my bedroom was a life-size head and shoulder picture of Ray and something very strange and sinister about it always puzzled me. One evening when I was about 5 years old, lying in bed, looking at this picture . . . it seemed to look straight back at me in a way that it never had before. Ray's eyes became real, her features alive and while I watched, it seemed as if Ray stepped straight out of the picture frame to my bedside. This was so unexpected that I was terror-stricken, and covered my head with the sheets, screaming with fear, which brought the entire family rushing into my room. All I was able to say was the "lady moved" but after they had managed to pacify me, they tried to prove I was mistaken by taking me to the picture, making me touch it and ensure that it was only a picture. As already stated, theory cannot alter fact and although I knew that it was only a picture, nothing could shake my conviction that Ray actually moved, in spite of all that was said to the contrary. This recurred on several occasions until I was in perpetual fear of the picture, so much so, that it had to be taken down and hidden out of sight. This removal, however, did not stop the spirit visitations and neither did my fears subside. We could stop to wonder for a moment whether God would start working by instilling fear into the heart and mind of a child!

It became evident that something was happening that could not be accounted for, and my grandmother was certain that the spirit of Ray was coming to me at nights for a special purpose and made up her mind that she was going to find out why. So she went to a Spiritualist medium, and the "spirit" of Ray becoming manifest, she was asked why she was coming to frighten me. She replied that she was only watching over me and did not realize she was making me so afraid. This should have made my grandmother decide at the time that the manifestation obviously was not from God, but it did not, and she did not give up Spiritualism. The medium had to explain to the "spirit" that she was dealing with a child who did not understand and she could watch over me without even showing herself. This seemingly did the trick, because I never had any more of these visits and I can only surmise that the demon who was impersonating Ray, just contented himself by watching over me and waiting his time.

Satan doesn't let us go as easy as all that, and although I wasn't troubled by such visitation for some time, it is evident that Satan was prepared to wait, having sown the seed in my young mind.

Having gotten over what was put down as nightmares by all except my grandmother, I could never really forget those experiences. My family was anxious that I should grow up to be a good Jew and I was taught the usual customs and ceremonies of Jewish family life. The Name of Jesus was never mentioned except disparagingly. I had heard that Jesus was a clever man who did wonderful tricks, and I also heard many derogatory remarks, poems and songs about Him which I just took in my stride and joined in the fun. It was the usual practice for my sister and me to go to the movies once a week—we weren't allowed to mix with Gentile children and this was our one relaxation. On one occasion, when I was about seven years of age, the film we saw was "The King of Kings" —the life and death of the Lord Jesus Christ. For the first time in my life I saw Jesus as a good man and so different from the way I had had Him described before that I cried nearly all the way through the film. Even at that age I realized that all the things I had heard about the Lord Jesus Christ were not true and this picture left its mark upon my mind. I dare to believe that the Lord was speaking to me through this film, although it was going to be some years before I would actually realize my need of a Saviour.

My parents at this time were very orthodox and saw to it that I was brought up to Judaistic ritual and teaching. Hebrew classes at the local Talmud Torah were the order of the day, where we learned what was expected of a good Jew. Separation from non-Jewish children was essential, although I was inwardly revolting against such ideas, especially as I considered that my teachers were untruthful concerning Jesus as I had seen Him portrayed in the film.

The strictness of Judaism became irksome and as I grew older, a query as to the necessity of such stringent behaviour arose in my mind. In the meantime, I had begun a serious study of music and was invited by my music teacher to practice on the organ of the church at which she was the organist (a non-conformist church). This was entirely unbeknown to my family. Before very long I was acting as official organist and choirmaster of this church, on Sundays, while still considering that being a Jew was also part of my duty. In the course of time, however, trying to keep pace with two religions became beyond me, and the opportunities arising in the church, to devote my time to music, soon overcame my family scruples and eventually I broke away from all Jewish ideas completely. Next came the bother of deciding whether I was a Jew or a Christian, but since by this time I had gathered a rough idea of the life of Christ, and what I knew I liked (purely from a humanitarian view point), I decided to call myself a Christian and from that time onwards, honestly tried to live up to the standards of life that I believed God expected from me. I had, of course, never had the Lord Jesus Christ presented to me as a personal Saviour, otherwise things might have been different. I was trying to live out a Christless Christianity, which so many people are attempting to do, but which, of course, is impossible.

When my Jewish birth was discovered, it became obvious that I was being cold-shouldered in the church where I was working and despite all my efforts to be a Christian, people would still remind me, in none too pleasant a way, that I was a Jew! I decided to leave this church and try to settle down in another church possibly of a different denomination. I had a strong inward yearning for something satisfying, but what that something was, I hadn't the remotest idea. The same kind of rebuff over my birth and parentage was met with, however, until I decided to give up altogether acknowledging the fact that I was a Jew, and when asked about it, replied in the negative and affirmed my "Christianity". This didn't help matters very much as my appearance gave me away and it was while I was feeling generally disheartened one evening, that the devil, who was waiting patiently to claim me for his service, found the opportunity at this very moment when I was at my wit's end. I was walking along one of London's streets, my mind very disturbed, not knowing what to do or where to go, when suddenly I actually saw a replica of myself standing in front of me! This was a strange experience, as in spite of my grand-parents' interest in Spiritualism, I myself knew nothing about it, which made it the more remarkable. Spiritualists would say that I saw my own etheric body, but whatever it was, Satan had stepped in to fill the gap that the Lord Jesus could have filled, had it not been for the fact that in the church today there are so many unfaithful and unprofitable servants who do not tell of the love that Jesus has for individuals and that His blood cleanses from sin. If I had known this then, I should not have been so aimless in purpose and empty of true spiritual life. However, here I was, having a psychic experience which I could not account for and as I saw this vision of myself, I remembered the picture of Ray and the visitation which frightened me when I was young. Now, I was older and fear did not enter my mind—it was rather astonishment! As I looked at this strange vision of myself,

the vision spoke and said "Follow me". Being ready
for any adventure, I followed, but as I set my foot for-
ward, I felt my whole body being lifted up. My mind
went completely blank and the next thing I remem-
bered was sitting in a small church where a woman
was speaking. This church turned out to be a Spiritu-
alist Church and this was the first time I had ever been
to a Spiritualist meeting. In spite of several references
made by my grandmother to Spiritualism, I had al-
ways ignored the idea of the possibility of the dead
communicating with the earth (in spite of my child-
hood experiences) and never went to any of their
meetings. Strangely enough, I was not surprised to
find myself at a meeting and was content to sit
through the whole service. When the speaker had
finished, it was announced that she would demonstrate
her psychic powers after the singing of the next hymn
(which was "Open my eyes that I may see"—a favor-
ite hymn before such a demonstration). This was sung
reverently and prayerfully and afterwards, the woman
stood up and pointed straight across at me sitting at
the back of the hall and told me my name. This sur-
prised me as I didn't know her at all—she then went
on to tell me that she knew of the strange experience
that I had just undergone, and added a description of
one of my music professors and commented on the re-
mark he had made recently concerning a new musical
composition which I had just completed. She told me
that I was a medium and had been watched by spirits
all my life. She reminded me of the spirit manifesta-
tion of my childhood and told me I was now old
enough to understand what they all meant. She elab-
orated on the situation, and said that God had seen
all my difficulties and had sent the "spirits" to come to
my aid and get me to the meeting. This seemed very

feasible to me then, and in view of the discouragement I had had from the churches (Christian) plus this remarkable experience, I decided to leave the church and become interested in Spiritualism. I went to seances, developed various types of mediumship and in no time was being received with open arms by the Spiritualists, who had no form of racial discrimination. What I was, what my views were, or anything else about me, didn't matter, just so long as I believed in the fact that spirits *could* and *did* communicate with the living; soon all doubts were lost, and I was being used in deep trance for the healing of bodies, for exhortation and other practices. Many bad cases of sickness came my way, and I really believed that in the healing of them, I had found what I was searching for, a knowledge of God. Visions and other psychic experiences became a natural, every-day occurrence.

War breaking out in 1939, I joined the British Army, serving for five years, and during this period of war service, preached Spiritualism to the men. Many converts to the Movement were gained in this way and I returned to active work in the Movement in 1945, after discharge. From then on I made investigations into all branches of the work, scientifically and spiritually, still trying to combine my ideas of the Christian religion with the ideals of Spiritualism—and considered that I was forging ahead spirtually speaking, eventually becoming ordained as a minister. I undertook much work through mediumship—but unfortunately (or fortunately) still was not altogether satisfied in my own heart—there was still a void!

It was a great desire of mine to "test the spirits" and the only way that I could see to do this was by their works and making them prove their identity. I happened to have one spirit "guide" pretending to be the spirit of a well-known European and I made up my mind that if I could get a man or a woman to come to the seance where this spirit was manifesting, who could speak the European language of the dead person the spirit was presuming to be, it should be able to prove itself. The spirit, however, did not agree and on another occasion, I invited a churchman to attend and converse with the spirit, but again the spirit refused to have anything to do with us, much to my annoyance. It did, however, agree to scientific testing where it was established that it was a definite entity that was manifesting and obviously not my subconscious self acting. This half-satisfied me, but I was still surprised that the spirit would not agree to testing in all respects.

One day I met a man claiming to be a Rational Spiritualist, that is to say, he believed neither in a personal God, nor in prayer or hymn singing. His oddest claim was that he was a master in black magic and that he knew that the spirits controlling him were evil spirits, but doing good work! He said that there were too many people calling themselves Christian Spiritualists, which was dishonest, as a Spiritualist obviously could not be a true Christian. This shook me a bit; he invited me to conduct a seance at his home for a test, but I was convinced that nothing would happen, since our viewpoints were so radically opposite. I was confident that my spirits were good spirits and his were evil. There would be no successful phenomena, since obviously they would not work in harmony. Since he was so persistent, however, that it should be put to the test and as I was just as anxious to test all things, we agreed on a set night to go to his home and conduct a seance before a reliable group of witnesses, who would be frank about the whole procedure. We decided that we would both go into trance condition and allow our "spirits" to communicate and see what happened. I was positive that nothing would happen—and he was certain that something would. I had visions of pandemonium during the seance! As will be seen during the following chapters, trance is a condition where the spirit takes full control of the medium's body and the medium knows nothing whatever about the procedure of the seance, having to be told of the results when he regains consciousness. That was the reason for the presence of reliable witnesses.

The evening duly arrived, and we met at the appointed place for the test. No hymns were sung, no prayer was given and we both went into trance. The seance lasted about an hour and when we both came out of the trance, the members of the seance were asked for their opinions and I was astounded to find that everyone agreed on it being a most spectacular seance. My spirit helpers were conversing with the other medium's helpers, and apparently they were all friends together. Several other seances followed, for some months, and similar results were obtained each time.

I became very concerned about the whole matter. Here was a man who did not believe in God as a personality, but believed only in dealing with evil spirits, a man who did not believe in prayer and hymn singing, but was still able to produce definite phenomena through his spirits and also to do good works. On the other hand, there was myself, spending a great deal of time in devotion and prayer and producing no better phenomena. It was all very puzzling. Was God answering my prayers or were they being answered by evil spirits? Was God working through this man and not evil spirits as he thought? What is the use of prayer and hymn singing? Where was God and where was He not?

During these months of mental confusion, I found that there was also a muddle amongst doctrinal points in Spiritualism. Some claimed to be Christian, while others did not; some believed in a God, while others did not. Some prayed, while others did not, and I began to wonder what I believed myself. As a Spiritualist minister, I was trying to reconcile Christianity with Spiritualism, even to the extent of quoting the Bible and explaining the miracles as mediumistic evidences. I had, until now, been quoting scriptures for many years, completely at random, but the idea was gradually dawning on me that God was not the Author of confusion. This led me to decide on making a search of the Bible and a tour round the different churches of all religions, to see whether I could find some common base in all of them to start building on, and which might yet supply the key to what I was still lacking.

Still holding on to the Spiritualist theory that the dead can communicate with the living, I began my tour through one church after another, which let me into Mormonism, Christadelphianism, Catholicism, Swedenborgianism and others, but I still could not find what it was that I knew must exist somewhere. The secret was within my grasp, but I had no idea where it was. "If only I might know where to find Him" was certainly the great yearning of my heart, yet, no one seemed able to tell me how to obtain it. I only knew that I was not satisfied and that the key was available, for the scriptures definitely say "Seek and thou shalt find". Not reading the scriptures in their entirety, I did not know what to seek—all I knew was that it was "truth" I wanted, not knowing that Jesus

said "I am the Way, the Truth and the Life . . ." the
spirits kept telling me not to be silly, as I already *had*
the truth, to give up fighting against myself and listen
to them and do as they told me, that by this way I
would eventually know all the truth. This did not alter
my mental struggles, and my determination increased
to find what it was that was devastating my soul. After
visiting church after church and meeting after meeting
I eventually came across a little Pentecostal Assembly
—not attached to any particular organization—and
decided that the following Sunday I would go to the
service there as I did not have a meeting of my own
that particular evening. The following Sunday, I ac-
cordingly turned up at the meeting (complete with
clerical collar) and as it was early, the members had
gathered together for prayer before the commence-
ment of the actual service. I heard some speaking in
tongues, while others interpreted and prophesied, and
began to think that I had walked into another Spiritu-
alist Church—only, although I was used to tongues,
interpretation and prophecy, etc. I felt that there was
a different atmosphere from what I had been accus-
tomed to in Spiritualist meetings.

Eventually the pastor came along to the platform
and the meeting commenced with chorus singing—
everyone appearing to be enjoying themselves. Possi-
bly, seeing the pastor striding up and down the plat-
form full of life and joy, and the members joining ex-
tremely heartily in the singing would normally have
made a newcomer wonder what he had wandered into
—but I was used to strange things and odd happen-
ings and took it in my stride. The pastor threw me sev-
eral glances and a welcoming smile—seeing that I was
a stranger—and after prayer and hymn singing, he an-
nounced that the Lord had burdened him to speak

that evening on "Spiritualism," which he announced and denounced as being "of the devil". During his discourse, he said many things that convinced me he knew nothing whatever about his subject—apart from the scriptural angle of it—and after the meeting he came over to me to give a personal welcome, and to ask if I were saved! I was not particularly interested in his views of "salvation"—but was highly incensed at his "presumption" in running down a Movement that he obviously knew very little, if anything, about. When I asked upon what authority he preached against it, he referred me to the Word of God—which suited me. I thought that we had equal ground here to start a logical discussion (I knew that I was acquainted with the scriptures of the Old Testament at least as well as he was—although I was not so sure of the New). We sat talking about the way of salvation until 11 p.m. that night, and in particular discussed the chapter much avoided by the Jews—the 53rd chapter of Isaiah. He asked me how, if the Bible was not the inspired word of God, this chapter could have been written about the Messiah 700 years before He appeared in the flesh? I argued that many people have been able to forecast certain events—men like H. G. Wells and Jules Verne—which have actually taken place since and that prophecy in no way proved the inspiration of the Scriptures. My contention was, of course, that they were merely a collection of the ancient historical writings of the Jews—not at all the very Word of God in the literal sense that it was now being expounded to me. I was then told that, although events could be forseen, it was not possible for one prophet to prophesy that one individual person would be born in such a manner, would live and die in such a manner as was predicted in this particular chapter. I argued again that possibly it could have referred to many other people besides Jesus of Nazareth in the course of history. After pointing out scripture after scripture referring to the birthplace of the Messiah and other details, he asked me if I could name some such person, other than Jesus, and he would grant me the possibility. Of course I was completely nonplussed and had to give in on that point. Granting the literal truth of this particular passage of Scripture and others in connection with the Messiah, naturally brought one to the conclusion that the other parts of Scripture were probably true also—including the ones referring to, and condemning, Spiritualism and such like practices. These particular references I had always put out of my mind, finding various excuses for not taking any notice of them (the blindness of the unbeliever is incredible)—or else had twisted certain incidents to fit in with spiritualistic ideas. Having to grant the possibility of the truth of these scriptures started me thinking, and although I was not converted that night, I was definitely experiencing a great mental battle with the spirits who controlled me, who were telling me that it was foolish to listen to such a man who had never been to a seance and could only argue from an old-fashioned Bible. However, I had to think this thing out for myself but my feet were at last on the right road—away from Spiritualism, and Satan.

Just after this conversation with the pastor, I attended what turned out to be my last seance, of which I was the acting medium, and during this event the controlling spirits attempted to take my life. I could not understand this at the time, but it has become evident since that they knew I was on my way out of their control and into a life controlled only by Christ. A couple of days after this incident, passing through

Westminster, I saw advertised at the Central Hall, a forthcoming convention to be held by the Elim Four-square Movement. During the period of my war service I was stationed near a small Elim Church, and always experienced a desire to go to one of their meetings. My spirits likewise counselled me to stay away, as it was not good for me to go there, and I had listened to their advice. This time I was determined to go, and on the 7th of June, 1947, I went and joined the crowd attending the meeting. I was still halting between two opinions, but remember that the very first hymn that was sung was "Blessed Assurance, Jesus is mine." I had never heard this hymn before and as the words were being sung, I could think of nothing else but the blessed assurance, Jesus is mine—and in a flash, realized through the working of the Holy Ghost that this was what I had been looking for. A blessed assurance —a sure knowledge that Jesus was mine—the result of a search lasting the best part of my life up to that time, an experience that I had gone my own way to find and had hitherto missed. While the congregation was singing the rest of the hymn I was asking the Lord Jesus Christ to save me in *His* way, and before the hymn was completed, I also had the assurance that I had come into a definite knowledge of salvation the scriptural way, through faith in the atoning *blood* of Jesus Christ, and was able to join in the final chorus "This is my story, this is my song, praising my Saviour all the day long," with my heart full of gratitude for the blessed assurance that the Lord had given. "Perfect submission, perfect delight, visions of rapture now burst on my sight, angels descending, bring from above, echoes of mercy, whispers of love."

Unfortunately, at the time of my conversion I had very little knowledge of the whole Word of God rightly divided, apart from the Old Testament which I had been brought up on, and half thought that now I had a personal knowledge of the Lord Jesus Christ as my Saviour, these "good spirits" would now work closer with me than ever before. However, to my surprise they stayed away completely! Strangely enough, I felt compelled by some inner leading to cancel all my connections with Spiritualism from the moment I became converted, although mentally I was not convinced against it. I also found that I was unable to fulfill any engagements to take meetings or seances, as it happened that I was prevented each time by some unexpected event, and never attended another spiritualist meeting from the day of my conversion. As I studied the Word of God more assiduously, my convictions as to the Satanic agency of these controlling spirits became stronger, and although I had no concrete proof at that time, I have had plenty since, that these communicating spirits are decidedly *not* of God.

After my conversion, a strong desire rose in me to be baptized in water—although no teaching had been given me in this respect—and was led very unexpectedly to a Baptismal service in Clapham which was being held in the open air on September 3rd, 1947. I applied to the pastor in charge and was able to follow the Lord through the waters of baptism—in a static water tank! On the 30th of September, 1947, the Lord graciously baptized me with the Holy Ghost, an experience not to be forgotten—speaking in other tongues, as the Spirit gave utterance. By this time I had convinced myself through the Word of God that spiritualism was definitely evil and that the spirits could not be what they purported to be—they were now to prove themselves for what they were! After receiving the baptism of the Holy Spirit, openings arose to testify in various assemblies and it was then that I came to realize the terrible strength of the Enemy of our souls. Evidently he had no intention of letting go his hold upon me as easily as I had thought. Each time I testified, attacks came in some way or another. Beforehand, dizzy spells made me so weak that I had to clutch something to remain standing up, let alone speak. After I had testified and had returned home, sleepy spells made me almost unconscious and my once familiar spirits attempted to get me into deep trance again, *against my will*—a thing they did not reckon to do, normally speaking. Several times they succeeded in using my own hands to attempt to strangle me. It was only by my standing upon the promises of God—defying Satan to do his worst—and by pleading the power of the Blood of Christ and by much intercessory prayer being given by the saints, that these evil spirits were eventually overcome. These attacks continued for some months, but the Lord is mighty and in His Name we conquered to the extent of complete deliverance. I know now what I am up against, and just how subtle the Devil is, but I know too that I am more than conqueror through Him that loved me enough to die for me—bless His wonderful Name for evermore.

I can truly say that the Lord has put a new song in my mouth—even praises unto Him—and I am devoting my whole life to the furtherance of His gospel and glory. The longing that I had all my life has been more than satisfied, and the half cannot be told of the blessing of His constant presence in my life—and still there's more to follow, praise His Name.

Thank God for the blessed assurance that He has given to me and can still give to whomsoever will come to Him. No longer do I need to seek satisfaction through the living to the dead, because I have found it in Him Who was dead, but is alive for evermore.

If I can do anything to convince people that Spiritualism is of Satanic origin, I will do so—and can only pray that the following chapters of this book will be used not only to arouse God's children to awake and meet the challenge which Spiritualism offers to us, with the power of the Holy Ghost and the weapons with which He has equipped us, but also to prevent people from inquiring into these things, perhaps only out of curiosity, which will lead them further and further away from God instead of nearer to Him, as so many are hood-winked into believing so sincerely.

CHAPTER II

THE SPIRITUALIST AND THE SPIRITIST

"Whatsoever thy hand findeth to do, do it with all thy might."

Ecc. 9, 10.

"I know thy works, that thou art neither cold nor hot, I would thou wert cold or hot. So then, because thou art lukewarm and neither cold nor hot, I will spue thee out of my mouth."

REV. 3, 15—16.

THE fact that the adherents of this cult apply the name of "Spiritualism" to their efforts to hold communications with the spirit world, has caused a great deal of consternation among the children of God. Many have stated that the term "Spiritualism" should be substituted by "Spiritism," seeing that it has no direct claims to true Christianity, even though a certain class among these people choose to call themselves "Christian Spiritualists" (with whom we shall deal in a later chapter). The term "Spiritist" is used by a child of God, when referring to all those who have dealings with, or take part in, the practice of any kind of psychic investigations. From this point of view, "Spiritism" is the correct designation, considering that the system is scripturally unspiritual and is obviously condemned by the Word of God. Denounce "Spiritism" to

any of these psychic investigators—deluded searchers
of truth—and much surprise would be aroused to find
that they would be in perfect agreement about it, be-
cause Spiritualists also denounce "Spiritism". Obvious-
ly there is some confusion of terms here. In order to
understand the reason for this apparent agreement
with the Christians' expressed complaint, it would be
advisable to view this subject from the angle of the
spiritualistic investigator and to discover the grounds
of mutuality when it is stated by both parties that
"Spiritism" is the "work of the devil."

From this point of view, then, what is a Spiritualist
and what is a Spiritist—wherein lies the difference?

Among the signs of the last days, we can see the re-
markable spread of Spiritualism, people giving heed to
seducing spirits and doctrines of demons and it is well
to constantly remember that *Spiritualism is an attempt
to communicate with what are presumed to be the
spirits of the dead. Those who indulge in this cult give
themselves up to demons, who pose as "spirit guides"
and "loved ones,"* and Spiritualists become ready to
give obedience to what are actually demons whether
they realize it or not. There are many reasons why
people start investigating into these mysteries and we
can sympathise to a certain degree with the many who
do so. For instance, some deeply and sincerely believe
that it helps them into a closer union with God, albeit
it is unobtrusively taking them away from Him. They
have no knowledge of spiritualism being forbidden by
God (Lev. 20:27) and that He considered such prac-
tices as criminal and worthy of death.

It does not take a child of God long, through the
revelation of the Scriptures, to realize that, although
many of the spirits in seances say gracious things
about the love of God, the God of the Spiritualists is

not the Holy One of Israel, but the "God of this world." *In other words, their God is really the "Prince of the power of the air, the Spirit who now works in the children of disobedience"* (2 Cor. 4: 4; Eph. 2: 2). Other parts of the Scriptures could be given in addition on these lines, but there are, of course, some Spiritualists who do not believe in the Scriptures at all—neither in a personal God. In view of the statements of Scripture which must remain the only measuring rod for all true Christians, there is only one conclusion that a Christian can arrive at, and that is that the spirits which so communicate, are *not* highly evolved "spirit guides" and the souls of dead persons, but actually *demons* impersonating dead people. This may sound strange and unreal to those who have had little or no contact with the principalities and powers of darkness, but to the student of Scripture, it is no new thing. In confirmation of the fact that the God of the Spiritualists is the "God of this world," a periodical called "The Banner of Light" issued on Nov. 4th, 1865, reported that "at a seance, the controlling spirit, through the medium, Mrs. Connant, was asked 'Do you know of any person we call the Devil?' 'We certainly do,' was the reply; "and yet this same Devil is our God, our Father!" The truth slips out in spite of themselves. "Ye are of your father, the devil" (John 8: 44). The demons, pretending to be the spirits of the departed, have to tread very carefully and they begin in a very plausible way and gradually ensnare those who are investigating out of mere curiosity. This type of people find something about Spiritualism that satisfies their love of adventure and although they may not have any intention in the first place of following this cult, it has been found that the mere giving in to this curiosity has brought disaster upon them.

Death has always been a universal foe and a curse which affects every home at some time—no one can escape it, all have to suffer the heart-ache of losing loved ones. It separates friend from friend, children from parents, husbands from wives, and inevitably leaves longing, aching hearts, especially if the bereaved is ignorant of the comfort and consolation of the Gospel of salvation through Christ. Consequently they are just the subjects for whom Satan is searching.

It is claimed that Spiritualists have the proof of survival, while the orthodox churches have only the faith in it. This is a point that lures many a church-goer away from the faith that was once delivered to the Apostles—the loss of the loved one and the query arising about the "other side." Surely the Word of God again comes to our aid—our faith is in Him Who conquered death and Himself appeared again afterwards to furnish the proof. Is it necessary for any to add to the finished work of our blessed Lord and Saviour? As we yield our life into His hands and He enters completely into it, there is no gap in the armor of faith that allows doubts and queries to creep in requiring us to seek additional proof through spirit seances. We know the He doeth *all* things well and are content to leave everything and everybody in His hands.

The bereaved one may cry like David, "but now he is dead, wherefore should I fast? Can I bring him back again? I shall go to him, but he shall not return to me" (2 Sam. 12: 23). Again at the news of the death of his son, we read that heart-rending-cry of a stricken father, "O my son Absalom, my son, my son." (2 Sam. 18: 33). Is not this the natural cry of one who has been separated from a loved one by the death curse? David, however, knew that in spite of his great grief, there was no possibility of making any contact this side of the grave with either of his children who had died; but there are so many others who are ignorant that the "dead know not anything" (Ecc. 9: 5). They want to know where their loved ones are, whether they are happy beyond the grave, whether they know that those left behind are thinking of them! Then while these thoughts are tearing at the longing, aching hearts of lonely people, Satan, through this Spiritualist movement, will say, "I know the answer, I can tell you where to find your loved one. I can tell you where you can communicate with him, where you can see him, speak to him and even touch him. He will be able personally to tell you how happy he is, and the interest he takes in you who are left behind. There need be no sting in death because it is all a delusion. *There is no death.*" Thus the poor ignorant sufferer is led away into darkness, giving a semblance of light, away from God, to be beguiled by the Serpent, with only one thought uppermost in his mind of seeing his love done again.

The reader may say that this is all just plain imagination and fraud on the part of the medium, and be inclined to judge the victims harshly as unbalanced or plain credulous, but if that is one's opinion, it is only because of the lack of knowledge of the subject! Many people are unaware of the challenge which Spiritualism presents to the true Church of God and they should be warned not to treat too lightly what is one of the most diabolical delusions that Satan is using in these last days. Spiritualism is not only a diabolical delusion, but also an awful reality, as many, including myself, are aware. Many have suffered greatly because they started investigating into this thing and have eventually been brought to distraction when they have attempted to free themselves from it. Homes have been broken up, suicide and lunacy have afflicted those who were once in it, and have dared to seek deliverance from its power. Those who have found that deliverance can only give thanks to God for His Grace and mercy.

There are, however, many thousands who have been unable to get free from the arch-fiend because they have never been told of the saving power of the Lord Jesus Christ. They are as unaware as if they lived in the depths of heathen lands, that if they call upon the name of the Lord they shall be saved. This seems incredible in this so-called Christian country, but is nevertheless a sorrowful fact.

Having touched briefly upon what Spiritualism really is, namely the contacting of demons who are pretending to be the spirits of the dead, we can now consider the actual difference between a "Spiritualist" and a "Spiritist" from the Spiritualist's point of view. As already stated, they will agree with the Christian's point of view regarding the fact that "Spiritism" is evil, and if asked to define what a "Spiritualist" really is, their answer would be three-fold:

(1) One who believes in life after death.
(2) One who believes in the possibility of contacting the spirits of the dead.
(3) One who considers it his duty to spread this "good news" to mankind.

As a former Spiritualist minister and active medium, it is possible for me to say that at the time of my participation in the Movement, I actually believed that these spirits were the spirits of the departed dead and that it was my duty to preach this to all those with whom I came into contact day by day. *It was my earnest desire that mankind should accept this "glorious truth" and find joy in the knowledge that there was no death.*

They believe that every person is a spirit that uses a body while on earth and when that physical body has completed its period of life on earth, it decays and eventually dies, leaving the spirit once again free to live on. They believe that once free from the body, the spirit is still a living, thinking, conscious individual who has a definite character and personality which makes it possible for it to reason things out. These spirits are supposed to be living a new life, but in spite of being bodiless, are still anxious for the well-being of those that are left on the earth.

Although their main beliefs are as previously stated, the most important being that there is no death, we must not overlook the fact that the average life of the sincere believer in Spiritualism is, in most cases, decent and honest—and as far as they know the meaning of the word, spiritual. They are sincere in their beliefs and maintain that they should be able to "give a reason for the hope that is in them." They also have a form of joy, which they think is the real thing, but it is very far from being joy, as realized by a Christian. Nevertheless, it is a very good counterfeit of the joy of the Spirit-filled child of God who has a knowledge of full salvation. *Spiritualists' joy lies in the fact that they have no need to fear death, whereas the powers of darkness have blinded their eyes to the real truth and have caused them to believe that they have a revelation direct from God.* They err because they know not the Scriptures and we, the true members of the Church of Christ, through His wonderful grace, need to pray for these victims of seducing spirits and rejoice when we hear that one has been delivered from what is, to-day, one of the most subtle forms of counterfeit that the Church throughout its whole history has had to face from the Enemy.

To a seeker after truth, it would appear that Spiritualism is the real thing, until faced with the reality of Jesus as a personal Saviour. Similarly, if one had a good imitation coin, believing it to be the genuine thing, it would be astonishing to find on comparison with a real coin, that the genuine one has a different ring. The genuine coin rings true, thus proving the falsity of the imitation. Such was my experience. I thought Spiritualism was true until, after testing Jesus and finding Him true, the falsity of Spiritualism became apparent. If only Spiritualists would taste and see that the Lord is good, they would be able to rejoice in the knowledge of sins forgiven through the precious blood of Jesus Christ and would make Him Lord of all. If we really seek truth, He is most certainly the rewarder of those that diligently seek Him, praise His Name, but we have to seek His way.

As previously stated, the joy of a Spiritualist is nothing compared with the joy of a born-again Christian. The joy of having such a Saviour, Who guides and keeps, far surpasses the joy conveyed by any teachers, or knowledge gained in Spiritualistic bypaths. Needless to say, Spiritualists maintain that they have a responsibility and that there should be no half measures in living up to the standards that are required. They have no time for the half-believer! To them there are no such persons as good or bad Spiritualists, a man is either a Spiritualist or he is not and if he claims to be one, he should be 100%. Half measures are definitely not believed in and recognition is not given to those who are lukewarm, neither hot nor cold. It is their united efforts to reach people that gain the interest of non-Christian organizations and, alas, of some professing but apparently not possessing Christians. It is grieving to see that, at a recent rally held in the interests of peace, at Caxton Hall, London, the Spiritualists were allowed to join in with Christian bodies and in the procession to Trafalgar Square which was an aftermath to the Caxton Hall meeting, led by a Salvation Army band and robed clergy. Many men well known in church circles also took part. The Spiritualists displayed a "prominent banner," to quote the *Psychic News*. Spiritualism makes every effort to reach the people by holding great open air meetings, healing campaigns, indoors and outdoors; miracles are being performed in the parks, etc.—is it any wonder that they are able to get their 3,000 converts a year (see chapter on History of Spiritualism) when such activity is going on and Satan is thus able to draw people by the thousands.

We can see from the above, that in their own estimation, these people have every right to call themselves "Spiritualists." "Spiritists" are, however, a great problem to the sincere worker and they term a "Spiritist" one who dabbles in the movement, attends meetings only to have a good time or to gain something for self, or just to get a message from the spirit world. Such a person would have no concern about spreading the message of "Life after death proved," although believing it, and would not be concerned about the welfare of mankind and would accordingly do nothing practical. They would have no interest in developing their own psychic gifts; their lives would be carelessly lived and wrapped up in themselves only, with no thought of perfecting themselves or of drawing others to the Movement—in order that mankind as a whole might eventually be led on to perfection.

The movement as a whole, both Christian (so-called) and non-Christian, utterly decry this type of person and contend that they would do better to dabble out, being no use to themselves, their fellow men, or the Movement in general. The conception of the Movement is much cherished by Spiritualists, pitifully so, considering that they are blinded victims themselves. Finally, Spiritualists regard "Spiritists" as being demon-controlled because of the amount of dishonor they bring upon what is considered to be "God's work." Would to God there were more 100% Christians in the church today, willing workers who would stop at nothing in order to bring to Christ the needy men and women that are all around us. God is seeking a people to-day who are prepared to sacrifice their all for His work; men and women who are willing to lay their lives on the altar and having done so, to leave them there without taking them back again.

Satan is demanding that people should worship him, but men love themselves too much to worship knowingly either the Prince of this world, or God. As a result, Satan has given the people something tangible in Spiritualism, which is not apparently Satanic, thus getting the worship that he requires indirectly, while our churches and even some of our ministers are either asleep or have come to the conclusion that Spiritualism is just nonsense. Are we to presume that God has taken so much trouble to warn His people, throughout His written Word, against such practices when actually it is but sheer nonsense? Are we to understand that God chose to mete out such penalties towards those who consulted or had dealings with one that had a familiar spirit when it is merely a harmless way of spending an evening? Yet this is the attitude of many of our church leaders to-day who sleep while Satan remains awake. We are able to see in these latter days, that while some of our workers sleep and others just pooh-pooh the subject, Spiritualism is spreading out its talons, the demons are working at top speed because they know their time is short, and our churches are fast falling into the clutches of the Enemy.

We know that in the same way as God uses the human vessel to work through, Satan does likewise, using the same persuasive eloquence that he used to beguile Eve in the garden of Eden. Satan will counterfeit even God's own methods by starting with the human vessel first.

Let the reader not think that Spiritualism is just sitting in the darkness all the time while spirits can be seen floating around the seance room and that there is nothing more attractive about it than that, because there is, to the one that is without Christ. It is fascinating in its doctrine, it is gripping and it is as real and actual as heaven and hell, but in spite of its fascination and apparent goodness, all its various branches of work are Satanic in origin.

There are, of course, two certain ways of discovering the truth about it—the testimony of those who have been delivered from it by the grace and power of God, and the Word of God. It is definitely not recommended that the reader should start attending seances to discover what goes on. If he does, he will find that he is walking right into a trap from which it is difficult to free oneself, no matter how strong minded one might be. *The way into Spiritualism is extraordinarily easy, the way out is extremely dangerous.* Christians have investigated into it a certain degree, but the knowledge gained has been costly and it is better to have truth revealed to us by God's own Spirit, in His way, rather than attempt to find such knowledge for ourselves.

Spiritualism offers many things to the soul without Christ—thrills, comfort, consolation, encouragement and advice, but it does *not* show the way of salvation, it does not lead the seeker to Calvary, only to utter darkness and a lost eternity.

Therefore, it should be avoided by the child of God, for the Scriptures make it plain that it is nothing more than faith in demons, substituted for the faith in God. We need to separate ourselves from this curse and touch not the unclean thing.

I was recently addressing a large meeting of Spiritualists and Christians combined, in a parish church in South London. The meeting was left open to comments by the congregation and it was remarked that since the Church had failed to do the works which Christ commanded us to do, God had raised up Spiritualists into a Movement to do them, and they *are* doing them (i.e., healings, etc.). From the Spiritualists' point of view this is a very logical statement, but how sad it is that we must agree that the church *has* failed to a very large extent in this respect and because this is so, Satan himself has been able to step in to do those very works—causing men and women to be caught by the tentacles of Spiritualism. It is my contention that if the Church were to stand foursquare on the Word of God, trusting itself to His leadership in the same way, and as entirely as Spiritualists do with their deceiving spirit guides, we would see those same miracles in as vast a measure, and greater besides, only effected by the hand of God and not the powers of darkness. We have to admit with shame that we fail God in our lack of obedience, but if Satan can do miracles through his mediums, surely God can do the same through us if only we stand upon His promises.

Let the Church take up this challenge of the enemy, let it awake and press on to the prize, let the assemblies be full of saints worshipping the Lord and magnifying His Name. Instead of resting on the past glories and revival days let us "prepare our hearts unto the Lord," thus making preparation for another revival in our time. Let the Church acknowledge God as the Great Jehovah and walk humbly with Him, let the prayer meetings once again be full of praying men and women whose one aim is to wrestle with God and do real business with Him, rather than to attend meetings for good times and happy chorus singing. These things have their place, but they must not be our ultimate aim in Christian service, which can only be the salvation of the lost and the glorifying of His Name. Spiritualism will remain a challenge to the Church until we are ready to fulfill the requirements of God; it will grow in mighty strength, snatching many precious souls from our reach, blinding men and women to the gospel of salvation, leading them into a Christless eternity. God forbid that we should, through our own lack of willingness and effort, be held responsible for the scarcity of converts and the blood of those we fail to reach be upon us!

Spiritualism has all the resources of Satan behind it, but we have all the resources of heaven at our disposal with the power of God behind and around us, and within us. We have the whole armor of God, loins girt about with truth, the breastplate of righteousness; feet shod with the preparation of the gospel of peace; the shield of faith, the helmet of salvation, and the sword of the Spirit, which is the Word of God.

Let us therefore pray with great supplication in the

Spirit and fight against the principalities, powers and rulers of darkness of this world and against this spiritual wickedness in high places.

CHAPTER III

THE HISTORY OF SPIRITUALISM

"In the latter times some shall depart from the faith, giving heed to seducing spirits, and doctrines of devils. . . ."
I TIM. 4, 1.

THOSE who approach this subject find it difficult to comprehend why the so-called spirits of the dead had to wait so long before being able to spread this "New Revelation" until, in fact, they could find two simple and uneducated girls in their early teens! We are told that many of these intelligences who are presumed to have passed on thousands of years ago, are supremely wise—that their main concern is to guide and uplift mankind, yet, in spite of their intelligence and their strong desire to do so much good, they were unable to do anything about it until 1848!

This delay on Satan's part was not due in any way to lack of demons to help in his work against the Church of Christ, for we are told that "Pheneas," the special control of the late Sir Arthur Conan Doyle's family circle, himself claimed to have died "thousands of years ago and to have lived before the time of Abraham at Ur." Another demon, a so-called guide who was the control of the circle of the Rev. Stainton Moses, preferring to call himself "Imperator," declared that he was identical with the prophet Malachi, 430 B.C.

It is difficult for any sensible minded person to reconcile the idea that these "high and exalted spirits" had to remain powerless for centuries before they could make their influence felt, but it is obvious that men like Sir Oliver Lodge, Sir Arthur Conan Doyle, and many other prominent men of learning were prepared to believe that this was so. It is still believed by men of learning to-day. They would even go as far as to say that the only hope of the human race is Spiritualism, which only shows how Satan has blinded their eyes.

Nevertheless, Modern Spiritualism or Rational Spiritualism (to differentiate between this branch and Christian Spiritualism which arose later, (see chap. IV), dates back only to the year 1848, and the anniversary is commemorated by large masses of people attending a meeting and demonstration. On the occasion, Sir A. Conan Doyle told a large audience at the Queens Hall on March 31, 1920, that they were gathered there that evening to celebrate the 72nd anniversary of what Spiritualists consider to be the greatest event which had occurred in the world for 2,000 years! Mr. Findlay, in his book, *The Rock of Truth*, says, "the real church is built on what man has discovered . . . its priests are the true interpreters of nature. Its Bible is the ennobling literature of the world, and its mediator betwixt earth and heaven is that gifted class of people called mediums, who can bring heaven to earth and unite the two worlds in one . . . all together will hold communication with the great and the good, the true and the noble, who have passed on, and who now come back willing and anxious to help us in our search for the truth and the real meaning of existence" (pp. 297-8).

In America, the frame house of the Fox family has been taken down and re-built elsewhere, bearing the inscription "Spiritualism originated in this house, March 31, 1848."

Margaret and Kate Fox were born at Hydesville, a little village about twenty miles from the town of Rochester, N.Y. It was a very poor district with houses of a humble type, mainly built of wood. Their parents were Methodists. There were other children in the family, but their names have no actual bearing on the subject. The whole of the Fox family took over the tenancy of the house in question on December 11th, 1847, and everything was apparently happy and uneventful until the middle of March, 1848, when sounds of knocking and furniture being moved were heard on many occasions, which frightened the children. At times the vibration was great enough to literally shake the beds. At this time Margaret was 14 years old and Kate was 11. Finally on the night of March 21st, 1848, young Kate challenged the unseen power to repeat the snaps of her fingers. The challenge was accepted and each snap was answered instantly by a knock, much to the surprise of the rest of the family. A contact with the unseen world had been established and the news spread around the village and far afield. Evidence was received that these spirits purported to be spirits of the dead, whereas in actuality, Satan had established a contact and had gained the confidence of the family and neighbors.

Many strange things happened—among others, Mrs. Fox's hair had turned completely white—and Satan established his foothold. Church ministers were seduced by the subtleness of the enemy under the guise of an angel of light. Many men of high character became interested in the strange phenomena taking place at the home of the Fox family and they spoke with sincere regard and sympathy of the two girls during their early years.

The girls became practiced mediums and for 30 years produced remarkable phenomena, but it is regrettable that these wonderworkers who for so long have been acclaimed as the founders of Spiritualism, came to a tragic end which we shall refer to again later.

It is recorded that the first message received through the Fox sisters was as follows:—

> "Dear friends, . . . you must proclaim these truths to the world. This is the dawning of a new era; and you must not try to conceal it any longer. When you do your duty, God will protect you and good spirits will watch over you."

Margaret and Kate Fox devoted all their energy to the propagation of Spiritualism, but the promised protection did not materialize and eventually they took to drink. In time they became victims of the drink menace, nothing could satisfy their craving for alcohol, and they lost all sense of moral responsibility. Margaret, in the presence of her sister Kate at an anti-Spiritualist meeting in 1888 declared, "I am here tonight, as one of the founders of Spiritualism, to denounce it as absolute falsehood . . . the most wicked blasphemy the world has ever known".

Within a few years they were both dead, Kate being the first to go. Spiritualism had sent them to their graves and Satan had not lessened his hold upon them.

An American newspaper described Margaret as an "object of charity, a mental and physical wreck, whose appetite is only for intoxicating liquors." It continues to say, "the lips that utter little else than profanity, once promulgated the doctrine of a new religion which still numbers its tens of thousands of enthusiastic believers." Kate is also reported as having said, "I loathe the thing I have been," and to those who wanted her to give a seance, "You are driving me to hell." Both died as a result of drink, and cursed God as they died. What a testimony from two who revived one of the oldest forms of heathenism known to men! How true it is that their end was as "bitter as wormwood, sharp as a two-edged sword." Their "feet go down to death," their "steps take hold on hell" (Prov. 5: 4, 5). How much better is it to fight the good fight of faith against all these principalities and powers, trusting in the God of all grace, Who hath called us unto His eternal glory by Christ Jesus, having fruit unto holiness and the end, everlasting life.

From the time of the Fox sisters, Spiritualism made very rapid advances, resulting in its spreading to many parts of the world by means of their missionaries. The most important woman from the point of view of British Spiritualists is Mrs. Hayden, who in the year 1852, accompanied by her journalist husband, a native of New England came to England. She was described as young, intelligent and at the same time simple and candid in her manner. The British Press, however, treated her as a common American adventuress; but although she met with a great deal of opposition, there were some who were prepared to throw all they had into championing the cause of what they thought was a newly found truth.

When Mrs. Hayden returned to the United States in 1853 and graduated as a Doctor of Medicine, she left behind her a handful of people to expound Spiritualism; among them the famous Dr. Ashburner, one of the Royal physicians. Mrs. Hayden had planted the first seed of this vile system right in the heart of London. News of the psychic events spread to Yorkshire, from Yorkshire to Lancashire. It was in 1855 that the first Spiritualist newspaper was started, at Keighly, called *The Yorkshire Spiritual Telegraph*. The expenses of this paper were met by a David Weatherhead, whose name is consequently honored among Spiritualists as being one of the first to throw himself wholeheartedly into the Movement.

Many different societies made their investigations into these strange affairs, including the Dialectical Society in 1869. In 1870, Sir William Crookes, the eminent scientist called upon men of science to investigate these remarkable phenomena which at that time were occurring with almost incredible frequency. He went so fully into the study of psychic phenomena that in 1874 there was talk of the Royal Society depriving him of his Fellowship, but this never happened, although from that time onward he was apparently more careful in the expression of his views.

The establishment of the British National Association of Spiritualists in 1873 encouraged many to join the ranks and learned and famous people supported the new Movement. In the meantime, Dr. J. R. Newton, a healing medium, famous in America, had arrived in England and extraordinary miracles were taking place. Free treatment was given and the sick clamored for healing through his power.

In 1881, another weekly Spiritualist newspaper, *Light*, was started, and 1882 brings us to the formation of the "Society of Psychical Research."

Spiritualism had, by this time, spread into many homes in Great Britain. At the same time it had gained ground in Germany, France, Italy and America. Various societies were formed, conferences held, large public meetings took place and many were swept into the new cult with blinded eyes, without perceiving that it was evil in its origin and would lead them only to destruction.

That Spiritualists themselves are, in the main, deceived into thinking that they are doing the work of God must be granted; hence the danger of such a movement which today is being propagated by sincere, earnest and good living people—themselves deceived by the arch-enemy of our souls—and no wonder, for miracles are wrought before their very eyes, limbs restored, sight given to the blind, sickness removed, and all as a result of their contact with "spirit guides." It is difficult, nay impossible, apart from the grace of God, to convince one who has been healed in some remarkable way through spirit agency that that very agency is demonic! It is well to remember that there shall arise false Christians and false prophets and shall show great signs and wonders, inasmuch that if it were possible, they shall deceive the very elect (Matt. 24: 24). One scriptural way in which Spiritualism definitely is "scriptural" is in its fulfilment of prophecy! *Rational Spiritualism denies the divinty of Christ, the atoning value of the cross, the existence of hell and a personal devil, the inspiration of the Bible and the fall of man.* At a conference held in 1866 at Providence, Rhode Island, U.S.A., at which 18 States and Territories were represented, the following resolutions were passed:—

    (1) To abandon all Christian ordinances and worship.

    (2) To discontinue all Sunday schools.

    (3) To denounce sexual tyranny.

    (4) To affirm that animal food should not be used.

amply demonstrating among this particular branch of Spiritualists the proof of I Tim. 4: 1-4. "In the latter times some shall depart from the faith, giving heed to seducing spirits and doctrines of demons, speaking lies in hypocrisy; having their conscience seared with a hot iron; forbidding to marry and commanding to abstain from meats. . . ." *Forbidding to marry refers to their teaching spiritual affinity,* whereby many happy homes have been broken up as a result of the teaching of spirits, that every one has a twin soul. The spirits even go so far as to introduce "twin-souls" to each other, after which introductions they are encouraged to leave homes, husbands, wives and children, to live together, because it is the will of a spirit guide. The marriage vow is entirely disregarded where necessary, and the result is immorality.

Although Spiritualists celebrate their anniversary as from 1848, they will also declare that it is an old religion and that the Fox sisters only started a revival of what was already known. They are, of course, quite correct! History tells us of the witch hunts, tortures, burnings, etc., which were in operation long before the Fox sisters started the Spiritualist revival, but now, instead of being referred to as witchcraft, it is known as Spiritualism in almost every household all over the country, where small home circles, called seances, are held by families and friends for the purpose of contacting the spirits of their loved ones.

The Israelites were corrupted by idolatry and witchcraft (see Lev. 19: 26, 31; Deut. 18: 10-14, and other Scriptures) which they had obviously contracted from surrounding nations. Not only were the children of Israel corrupted but the pernicious doctrines have since spread throughout the world.

During the Dark Ages, astrology, demonology,

magic and necromancy, etc., became really rampant in Western Europe and England. From the 14th to the 17th centuries, witchcraft spread surprisingly throughout the Continent. The bad weather of the spring of 1556 was blamed on the witches, and the Archbishop of Treves was instrumental in the destruction of 118 witches and wizards. During the Spanish Inquisition, 30,000 people were burnt as witches and strange things happened during these times that were indisputably attributable to disembodied spirits. Superstition alone could not have produced the manifestations that history has recorded.

Numerous Acts were passed at different times by Parliament in order to stamp out the curse of witchcraft, beginning with one in the time of Henry VIII, in 1530, but the main ones being the Witchcraft Act of 1735, which will be referred to later on in this chapter.

Three of the leading societies at the present time are The Spiritualists National Union, whose Headquarters are in Manchester; The Marylebone Spiritualist Association, whose offices are at Russell Square, London, (the total membership of these two societies is roughly 44,000); and The Greater World Christian Spiritualist League, which will be discussed separately in the following chapter.

The Spiritualists National Union has nearly 500 churches and 18,000 members and was founded in 1891. It declares that its President is the spirit of the late Sir A. Conan Doyle. Although it does not claim to be Christian, it has no objection to its members calling themselves Christians if they so desire, providing that they agree with the seven principles of which every one of their churches must approve before being allowed to enter into fellowship with the Union. These principles are:—

(1) The Fatherhood of God.

(2) The Brotherhood of man.

(3) The communion of saints and the ministry of angels.

(4) Human survival of physical death.

(5) *Personal* responsibility to answer for one's own sins.

(6) Compensation or retribution for good or evil deeds.

(7) Eternal progress of every soul.

The Union claims that all these principles, with the exception of the fifth, are compatible with ordinary Christianity. Our Lord's life and death is looked upon as an example only. Redemption through His Blood does not come into their teaching, and it is believed that every man answers for his own sins. *Sir A. Conan Doyle states that "none can shuffle out of that atonement by an appeal to some vicarious sacrifice."* The President continues: "It is not possible for the tyrant or the debauchee, by some spiritual trick of so-called repentance, to escape his just deserts. A true repentance may help him, but he pays the bill just the same." The President apparently placed no weight on Romans 8, 1: "There is therefore now no condemnation to them which are in Christ Jesus, who walk not after the flesh, but after the Spirit." However, the Union allows for a wide interpretation of its tenets and shows a certain amount of tolerance and grace towards the individual opinions of members who are nearly all voluntary workers and recognized ministers. Only a few full time professional mediums get a fee. The mediums belonging to this Union must have good recommendations from their church and if they wish, they may be allowed to enter for an examination by giving demonstrations under very strict conditions of testing, and by satisfying the judges of their knowledge of psychic matters. A much prized diploma is issued to the successful candidate.

The Marylebone Spiritualist Association, founded in 1872, holds seances and gives private sittings to enquirers and believers in their building in Russell Square. There is a medium in attendance with the gift of healing, who together with a band of willing workers is available to assist people suffering from different complaints. A great deal has been done in this respect. A Sunday meeting is held regularly at the Victoria Hall, where an approved medium demonstrates Clairvoyance (i.e., a clear seeing of spirits) to a packed hall holding 800 people, the majority of them anxious to receive some message of hope and comfort from the medium, who is just as anxious and willing to satisfy their needs.

Any assistance or advice is freely given to all in genuine need, but a fee is normally charged for sittings with mediums. One can become either an Associate or a Member of the Association after signing a declaration that one is either a seeker or a believer in Spiritualism. Their aims and the work that they do are explained in their brochure which can be obtained free of charge; it states:—

"This brochure is intended for inquiries into Spiritualism in its highest form, covering investigation of survival after death, communication with the spirit world, psychic phenomena, the desire for spiritual development and the search for truth in many directions. The purpose of the M.S.A. is to provide an organization through which these attributes may be vigorously pursued, and a center where workers from the spirit world may bring proof of survival, comfort, healing and instruction to its members and help them to realize their essential unity with the spirit world. Spiritualism is not antagonistic to any religious belief and therefore the M.S.A. is entirely non-sectarian and membership is open to all."

Incidentally the point of whether Spiritualism is contrary or not to religious beliefs is a moot point not altogether accepted by the leaders of the Church in this country. In this respect, it may be as well to mention the controversy caused by the investigation into Spiritualism by a Committee nominated by the Primate, the Archbishop of Canterbury, Dr. Lang, in 1937. It is advisable to bear in mind that he instituted this Committee after agitation had been set up by several well-known members of the clergy, who considered the time was ripe for the Church of England to investigate the Movement. The Committe did not confine itself to investigation of evidence submitted by Spiritualists—they considered the views of witnesses unfavorable to Spiritualism, they went in a body to seances, asking questions of mediums and the "spirits" who manifested through them, and embodied their findings into a report which was duly returned to the Archbishop of Canterbury and was presented to the Archbishops and Diocesan Bishops of England. It was not made public.

This was certainly not what Spiritualists had expected, especially as they understood from admittedly unauthorized sources that the report was favorable in the main to their Movement.

Three leading Spiritualists wrote to the Archbishop of Canterbury to know when the report would be made public. The reply was given by the Primate's Chaplain to the effect that when the report came up for review it was felt that further investigation was needed and that premature publication would be liable to give rise to misunderstanding, therefore it would not be published at that time.

Simultaneously, the Editor of the *Psychic News* (the Spiritualists' newspaper with the world's largest circulation) approached Dr. Underhill (chairman of the Committee) stating that allegations were being made that the report was being deliberately suppressed because it presented Spiritualism in a favorable light. Dr. Underhill replied that the report disclosed much difference of opinion and it was consequently felt that there was need of further careful investigation. On that account it was decided that the report should not be made public.

Prominent Spiritualists continued to agitate for the release of the report, the Archbishop of Canterbury maintaining the resolve not to publish it. It was stated in reply to another letter from a Spiritualist that the report had been private and confidential, submitted to him and his brother bishops on the subject of Spiritualism and it would be reconsidered as to whether it should be made public. Evidently the 41 diocesan bishops decided on its being kept private as it was never published at all.

Whether the decision was a wise one or not—and presumably the bishops had the laws of God in mind and the knowledge of resulting chaos if they made a decision giving the Church members a wrongful lead —it gave an incentive for Spiritualists to claim that a great wrong had been done to them in the suppression of "truth" by a hide-bound orthodoxy. The Psychic Press published a book on the subject giving all available data of the Committee, the correspondence between one and another, colored, of course, by their own viewpoint.

Much ado was made about the report being favorable to Spiritualism, yet they seemed to see nothing incongruous in the fact that several members of this investigating Committee already had spiritualistic backgrounds—the chairman is a psychic, another member has devoted a quarter of a century to psychic research and has revealed that he is his own automatic writing medium. Taking this into consideration, it is not surprising that the report should be "favorable." It would have been far more surprising if it had not been!

Although Spiritualists have only gained State recognition comparatively recently, they are growing in numbers, and it is recorded that they are getting 3,000 converts a year. Before they were recognized as a "religion" there were many prosecutions of mediums suspected of fraud, and even in recent times I have known of genuine mediums being sent to prison for fraud. The reason for these prosecutions is in the fact that under the Vagrancy Act of 1824 and the Witchcraft Act of 1735, a medium could still be prosecuted until recently. These Acts state that a person has committed an offence if they either conjure up spirits or even pretend to be able to do so. Consequently they were caught both ways as once a medium was charged under the Vagrancy Act or the Witchcraft Act they were liable to be punished either for being frauds and pretending to conjure up spirits or for being literally able to do so, if fraud could not be proved. Under such conditions the Spiritualist Movement as a whole was bound to keep within the law although the Home Secretary promised at one time that mediums would be left alone if there was no reason to believe that an element of fraud existed. Obviously then Spiritualists had to be careful in the choosing of their ministers and mediums. We have to grant that though they are deluded, they are sincere in their beliefs and their recently granted "freedom" will no doubt only add to their care in choosing their mediums since they will get wider publicity. Meetings held in small churches or halls are open to the public, and anyone entering will receive a warm welcome from the members or officers. The usual form of the service is on the lines of a Free Church; there is hymn singing, prayer, and sometimes a Bible reading. The visiting medium usually gives an address and at the close of the service will give a demonstration of clairvoyance.

Their churches are invariably all well-attended, they have their own Sunday Schools (called Lyceums) and young people's meetings, but young people are not allowed to become members of the Union until they have reached the age of 21.

Spiritualism is now attempting World Federation and such societies as the Universal Brotherhood Federation aim high in order to achieve this end. Its founder, Mr. Noah Zerdin, apart from organizing large indoor meetings, has also instilled enthusiasm into other Spiritualists who voice their teachings and principles at Speakers Corner in Hyde Park. The *Psychic News*, in their issue of October 20th, 1951, states: "In Rome last April at a convocation of World Federal Movements, drawn from 55 nations, three U.B.F. delegates were present, Noah Zerdin, Ben Herrington and Leo Bliss." These three energetic workers are all out for Spiritualism and when they are silenced, they set to work with the pen and wherever an opportunity presents itself Zerdin is ready to speak on behalf of Spiritualism. The Universal Brotherhood Federation aims at World Federation Government, World Food Board, a World Bill of Rights to protect the individual citizen and punish the violators of world laws, and a world Police Force. Such is the work being done in the Spiritualist Movement today and if we were as undaunted as Mr. Zerdin and other workers in the Movement, ready to speak for our Lord, ready to testify of His never-failing love, ready to take up the pen when silenced, we would see the hand of God moving among His people, convicting the world of sin, of righteousness and of judgment. We would see real Holy Ghost conviction, men and women weeping their way to Calvary, admitting the Lordship of the King of kings. Instead of World Federal Government, etc., the government shall be upon His shoulders and He shall rule over His people.

No doubt Satan would prefer the government to be upon *his* shoulders, thus destroying the true church. He would deceive, if he had his way, by posing as a wolf in sheep's clothing.

Thank God, in spite of Satan's probable preference, it is *not* possible for his deceptions to last forever and his power is "but for a season."

Neither can any child of God be deceived, *while* their trust and confidence is in Him, Who is the Father of Lights.

CHAPTER IV

CHRISTIAN SPIRITUALISM

*"Not every one that saith unto me, Lord, Lord, shall enter
the Kingdom of heaven."*

MATT. 7:21.

THIS branch of the Movement believes—as all branches
do—in the ability to make contact with the dead.
While their seances take the same form, producing
similar phenomena as do the Rationalists, this part of
the cult is more satisfying for those who still prefer a
certain amount of orthodoxy and more colorful
churches, with altars, crucifixes and statues of Christ or
the Virgin Mary.

Although their beliefs are the same inasmuch as
they agree on fundamentals, they claim to be Chris-
tians as well as Spiritualists and although recognizing
that the Movement as it is known today, was revived
in 1848, they claim also that the phenomena experi-
enced in seances are identical with events that took
place while the Lord Jesus was in the flesh. They be-
lieve that Jesus of Nazareth was the Son of God, that
He was born of a Virgin according to scriptural proph-
ecy and that He was the Jewish Messiah. Special em-
phasis is placed on the Leadership of Christ and His
redemptive power (this latter not by the blood offer-
ing which is necessitated by a death to atone for sin,

but by a love offering which by His example draws men to God, thus making Him the Saviour of the world).

In recognizing the necessity of the new birth according to John 3:3, they hit very near the mark when they state that a man is born again when he makes up his mind to live a good life with Christ as an example, which they consider necessitates him making retribution for past deeds. The really born-again reader knows that these things automatically follow conversion, but our good lives are not necessarily a sign that we are born again. This only comes by first, a genuine repentance; second, an acknowledgement of the fact that in spite of our "good works" we are hell-deserving sinners; and, thirdly, by accepting the Lord Jesus Christ as our personal Saviour, our substitute. We know that when we are born again we become new creatures in Christ Jesus, that by His precious *blood* we are redeemed, for it is the blood that atones for the soul. Old things are passed away and having confessed our sins and repented of them, we are given the power to overcome and the grace to make restitution where possible.

Christian Spiritualists also believe in water baptism and some meet on the Lord's Day to break bread. The fact that Jesus shed His blood is only recognized as a natural outcome of death by crucifixion. They regard the power of Christ to be in His love for mankind and it is with this attitude of mind that they meet for breaking of bread.

Their church service takes place in the usual manner, with a demonstration by a medium at the end. They believe in prayer and devotion, and like other Spiritualists they have a warm and friendly welcome for strangers and inquirers. Their meetings are conducted reverently and prayerfully, and it became a matter of great concern to me when, as a Spiritualist, I found that in spite of my longer prayers I achieved no better results than other mediums who did not believe in prayer. It became a matter of even greater concern when I discovered a medium who did not believe in God at all and said openly that his "spirit guides" were evil spirits yet he had successful phenomena and good works without any aid from prayer at all.

Healing is regarded as a very important part of the Christian Spiritualist's ministry and is looked upon as a gift of the Spirit, in the same way as all the other eight gifts, which they consider to be in operation among their members (all of which are very cleverly substituted for the real thing by Satanic agency).

It can be seen how deadly Christian Spiritualism is to the true Church of Christ. It is one of my main regrets that I was blinded by the Devil with such subtlety and it is even more regrettable that in none of the different denominational churches which I went into at various times did I ever hear that the Blood of Jesus Christ could cleanse from sin. It is the faithlessness in preaching in many of our churches in these latter days that hinders people from getting a true knowledge of salvation. We can indeed praise God that there is still a section of the Church of Christ which is preaching the "full gospel" and standing four-square on the Word of God.

Sad to tell, many are being deceived by the names of these Spiritualists—so-called Christian—and many well known Christian Church leaders are today active Spiritualists, contrary to the will of God. Scripture (i.e., the Word of the Living God) is very definite on this point, e.g., Lev. 19:31; Lev. 20:6; Lev. 20:27; Deut. 18:10;11; Isaiah 8:18-20.

The Rev. H. P. Hawies, M.A., in an address before the London Spiritualist Alliance on April 20th, 1900 said that he had come there to say that he did not see anything in what he believed to be true Spiritualism, in the least contrary to what he believed to be true Christianity. We can thank God that we do not have to worry about what people believe to be true, but rather we can accept what the Word of God says regarding these things. It is difficult to reconcile the Scriptures and the practices of Modern Spiritualism, be it termed Christian or otherwise, in spite of people's opinions!

The Rev. Arthur Chambers, formerly Vicar of Brockenhurst, Hants., is reported as having said: "As a Christian Spiritualist I have one great hope, one great conviction of what will be, viz: that Spiritualism which has done so much for Christian teaching and for the world at large in scaring away the bugbear of death, in helping us better to realize that which a magnificent Christ really taught, will recognize fully what that Christ is, in the light of spiritual verities."

The Rev. F. F. Fielding-Ould, M.A., in an address on "The relation of Spiritualism to Christianity," on April 21st, 1921, stated, "the world needs teaching of Spiritualism." We must admit that the Church needs teaching on this cult, that they may know the truth, and the Devil may be exposed in his deception.

The Rev. Charles Tweedale, who labored in the cause of Spiritualism at the Bishops' Conference at Lambeth from July 5th to August 7th, 1920, says in *Light,* issued on October 30th, 1920: "While the world at large has been filled with an eager awakening interest, the Church, which claims to be the custodian of religious and spiritual truth has, strange to say, until quite recently turned a deaf ear to all modern evidences bearing upon the reality of that spiritual world which it is the main object of her existence to testify, and even now is only just showing faint signs that she realizes how important this matter is becoming to her. . . ."

Dr. Elwood Worcester, in a sermon entitled "The Allies of Religion," delivered at St. Stephen's Church, Philadelphia, on February 25th, 1923, spoke of psychical research as the true friend of religion and a spiritual ally of man. Another Church dignitary stated that Spiritualism makes a Jew a better Jew, a Mohammedan a better Mohammedan, a Christian a better Christian, and certainly a more happy and cheerful one!

The leading organization on the Christian side of Spiritualist churches was founded in 1931 and is called the "Greater World Christian Spiritualist League" with over 500 churches and 27,000 members. They preach what they hold to be the "true" gospel. Missionary services are held in public halls at which "Zodiac" (who claims to be the spirit of a teacher in the Temple at the time of our Lord's dwelling in the flesh) gives the address. Meetings have been held all over Great Britain, and in Canada, America, Paris, The Hague and the Channel Islands. Missionaries have also been sent to America, Australia, Tasmania, Canada, New Zealand, South Africa, India, Syria, Palestine, Belgium, France, Holland, and Switzerland.

The Greater World Christian Spiritualist League have their own weekly paper called *The Greater World*, and a young folk's monthly newsletter. Editions of *The Greater World* were prior to the War issued in French, German, Dutch, Arabic, Portuguese, Esperanto and some Indian languages. For some time this League has been instrumental in sending and giving food, clothing and money to the poor and the aged. Two free night-shelters for homeless women and a free convalescent home are entirely supported by the readers of *The Greater World*, and the League makes no compulsory fees in connection with any branch of the work of *The Greater World*.

I have chosen to make this known to readers, not from a point of view of supporting the ideals of the "Greater World Christian Spiritualist League" but in order that an unbiased opinion can be obtained of this society which we must admit is doing "good works." It can also be seen how the enemy of the true Church is out to deceive, if possible, the very elect, and to gain the admiration of the less wary. The principles of the League are allowed a fairly wide interpretation by its members—and so are the scriptures—and they look on lesser organizations with love and pity if they do not accept the Leadership of Christ.

The Greater World League have their own nine clauses and many of their churches make a practice of reading them at their Sunday services. They are as follows:—

(1) I believe in One God, Who is Love

(2) I accept the Leadership of Jesus Christ.

(3) I believe that God manifests through the illimitable power of the Holy Spirit.

(4) I believe in the survival of the human soul and its individuality after physical death.

(5) I believe in the communion with God, with His angelic Ministers and the soul functioning in conditions other than the earth life.

(6) I believe that all forms of life created by God intermingle, are interdependent and evolve until perfection is attained.

(7) I believe in the perfect Justice of the Divine Laws governing all life.

(8) I believe that sins committed can only be rectified by the sinner himself or herself, through the redemptive power of Jesus Christ, by repentance and service to others.

(9) I will at all times endeavour to be guided in my thoughts, words and deeds by the teaching and example of Jesus Christ.

From a fuller explanation of these clauses (which can be read in their booklet "Belief and Pledge of the Greater World Christian Spiritualist League"), it will be seen that the fall of man is denied, and the mention of Satan and his host of fallen angels is carefully avoided.

An assertion is made that animals have the same eternal souls as human beings. Belief is held in a second chance, whereas we are told by the Word of God that it is given unto man once to die and after death the judgment. The finished work of Christ is not considered sufficient to redeem man but salvation depends also upon our "good works," whereas the written Word once again tells us that salvation is not of works, lest man should boast. We can conclude that Satan is at the bottom of the "good works" which appear to be so divinely inspired and done with such good intentions, but which in reality are duping Spiritualists into believing that they are on the right road, whereas unfortunately they are very far from it.

It challenges the Church of Christ again to awake and pray to the Lord for a revival of His Church and that men and women shall be raised up who will stand on the Word of God and live according to His Will, as many have done in the past and are still so doing, although their ranks will stand a mighty increase.

The twisting of Scripture or giving it such a much wider interpretation than it was ever intended to have, is sufficient in itself to condemn any movement that uses it in this way . . . "If they speak not according to this Word, it is because there is no light in them . . ." (Isaiah 8:20).

CHAPTER V

THE LYCEUM

"Feed my lambs . . ."

JOHN 21:15.

Most Spiritualists have their own Sunday Schools which are called Lyceums, this being the name given by the founder of this system of teaching—Andrew Jackson Davis.

Andrew Jackson Davis was born in 1826 in Orange County, New York. His father was a leather worker who was addicted to strong drink, his mother was superstitious and uneducated, which is tantamount to saying that he was brought up in a difficult environment. He was weak in body and had very little learning. It is another remarkable point that the spirits had to wait so long before they could find an uneducated boy, brought up by a drunken father and a superstitious mother before they were able to found what Spiritualists claim to be the finest teaching system that it is possible to have, namely, the Lyceum.

It became evident that in his late teens, some power had overshadowed him, for he was suddenly capable of writing a book on philosophy, which caused quite a stir considering that up to the time he was sixteen he was only known to have read one book!

Satan apparently called A. J. Davis to his service

when he heard voices of demons (which he mistook for angels) calling him one day as he walked across the fields. These voices began by giving him advice and comfort and he very soon developed into a strong "psychic" under the teaching of a local medium, named Levingston, who incidentally was a tailor. It became evident that Davis was developing a power of medical diagnosis among his other psychic faculties. He was able to describe how a human body became transparent to his eyes so that each organ stood out clearly, while the affected organ became dim. I myself had this power of X-ray vision and was able to discover certain cases of bone trouble through this type of mediumship. In fact, these discoveries proved so correct that at one time I was offered employment by a doctor to assist in diagnosis, which I declined, not wishing to commercialize a gift. It is, however, a very real power.

On March 6th, 1884, Davis was suddenly possessed by the spirits while in trance—his etheric body was taken on a rapid journey from the town of Poughkeepsie where he was living, to wild mountains where he found himself talking to Swedenborg (at this time the latter was deceased). From then onwards he received many messages by clairaudience, which told him to go to the Catskill Mountains apparently for further communion and teaching from the spirit impersonating the deceased Swedenborg.

Sir A. Conan Doyle suggests that this calling to the mountains has some analogy to the experience of Jesus on the mountain when Moses and Elias appeared to speak about His death.

Davis was not religious, although he was certainly honest, earnest and anxious for the truth. However, he blindly refused to seek it the scriptural way, believing in the inspiration of his "spirits" rather than the Word of God. He progressed as a medium, developing among his many psychic gifts, the power to prophesy and before he was thirty, he was able to prophesy in detail the coming of the motor car and the typewriter. He writes in his book "The Penetralia," that "there shall be carriages and travelling saloons on country roads—without horses, without steam, without any visible motive power, moving with greater speed and far more safety than at present." He also claims in one of his visions, to have seen graduated phases of spiritual life where the studious can study, the artist can find art, lovers of nature can find beauty, and the weary can find rest. Such was the "revelation" he had of the after-life. During these spiritual travels through what he refers to as "the spheres," he says he learned that the object of life was to qualify for advancement, the best method to his way of thinking being to get away from sin. There is, of course, no mention of the atonement that can be obtained through the precious blood of Jesus Christ!

Davis was a man who lived up to his ideals and although he was poor he was charitable and patient in argument. He spent the last years of his life as a book storekeeper in Boston, where he died in the year 1910 at the age of 84—without Christ. God was certainly gracious in allowing this man to live well past his allotted time, giving him an opportunity of coming to a saving knowledge of the Lord Jesus Christ, which, however, he never did—Satan held him fast and with demon-blinded eyes this grand old man, who had grown from an uneducated boy, passed into eternity without a Saviour.

Davis left a mark upon Spiritualism when he founded the Lyceums. He claims to have been taken to the

"Summerland" (which he called the children's sphere) and there he saw spirit forms of children at the "Spirit world school." The teaching in the Lyceums is based on this vision which he described on January 25th, 1863, at Dodworth's Hall, Broadway, New York. He described the methods used for teaching the spirit children, and his descriptions of child life in the Summerland so impressed the Spiritualists gathered at that meeting that it was decided to start straightway by forming a Lyceum at the very hall with Davis as its Conductor.

He taught that the spirit world Lyceums meet in large halls with spacious surrounding gardens, that they know no sorrow, pain, poverty or hunger. They grow up into adults just as earth children do and increase in wisdom and stature. American Spiritualists decided to use the same system of teaching as Davis saw in his vision. The actual vision will be dealt with later on, but in the meantime we will take a brief look at the Lyceum from an historical aspect.

After the formation of the first Lyceum with A. J. Davis as the Conductor at Dodworth's Hall, other Spiritualists followed the idea, but the name of Mr. J. Burns is regarded as important by British Lyceumists as he was the first to introduce the system in England, which resulted in a Lyceum being opened at Nottingham in 1866, the conductor (leader) being Mr. J. Hitchcock, and within four years two more were started at Keighley and Sowerby Bridge in 1870. Several more sprang up in various parts of the country and in 1884 the first meeting of Lyceum workers took place at Bradford when delegates of the Yorkshire district of Spiritualists and other interested people attended. At that meeting it was agreed that "all workers in Lyceums should meet in conference every year to discuss the furtherance of the Lyceum Movement; also for material encouragement in the work." The next meeting took place in 1886 with Albert Kitson as Chairman. It was then moved that conferences should be held in different places which again resulted in the 3rd annual conference taking place at Leeds in 1887, when H. A. Kersey was elected President.

The names of Alfred Kitson and Harry August Kersey are regarded with great esteem by modern Lyceum workers as being pioneers in the Movement.

Alfred Kitson was born on February 15th, 1855, and was the eldest of six children with a father who was unable to carry on with his work as a miner owing to ill-health. Alfred, being the eldest, had to keep house and nurse the remainder of the children while his mother went out to work. When he was nine years old he went to work in the mines himself and was first introduced to Spiritualism when he was twelve years old, when he discovered that his father had joined a home circle—had become a medium (which eventually led to his healing by "spirit power" and he was able to resume work again).

Alfred Kitson started attending Spiritualist meetings and in 1871 he was appointed as the Conductor of the Gawthorpe Lyceum. Although he had not had much schooling he studied geology and became a reliable teacher. Together with H. A. Kersey and Mrs. Emma Hardinge Britten, he played a great part in the compilation of the first "Lyceum Manual" which is claimed as the rock on which Lyceumism is built. His book "Outlines of Spiritualism for the Young," is regarded as a classic by Spiritualists and A. J. Davis remarked about it as "in a word, the clearest and most comprehensive of any work of its pages that I have yet seen and it should be in the possession of every reader of progressive literature". Kitson attributed a great deal of his work to the co-operation of his wife and daughter Mary (who became Bachelor of Arts and also Secretary to the Education Scheme which started in 1920). He devoted his life to the work of the Lyceums and is regarded as the father of the British Spiritualists Lyceum Movement, dying without Christ on the 1st of January, 1934.

Kitson met Kersey at Newcastle in 1886 and this first meeting resulted in the formation of the Lyceum in that town. Kersey at his own expense prepared the "Spiritual Songster" which is used in Lyceums and which he later presented to the Union together with the Lyceum Manual for which he also paid. He did a great deal in raising a publishing fund and also in organizing the Lyceums into districts with their own district visitors.

The name of another who ranks as a pioneer of the Lyceum Movement is Mrs. Emma Hardinge Britten who was born in 1823. She went to America in her late twenties and stayed there until 1864; it was there that she came into contact with Spiritualism and it was not long before she became noted as an expert on the subject touring Canada and the U.S.A. giving lectures. As soon as she arrived back in England she was acknowledged as a leader in the Movement and devoted all her energies to the work, among other things writing a 16 page pamphlet for the use of Lyceum sessions, and playing an important part in the preparation of the Lyceum Manual. She died on the 2nd of October, 1899.

The first constitution of the Lyceums was accepted by the workers in 1890 and the "Spiritualists' Lyceum Union" was formed. Its title was changed in 1894 to the "British Spiritualists' Lyceum Union." 1890 also saw the publication of the *Spiritualists Lyceum Magazine* which a few months later was superseded by the *Lyceum Banner* adopted on May 10th, 1891, as the official organ of the British Spiritualists Lyceum Union. Kitson took over the editorship of the *Lyceum Banner* in 1902 and also acted as it's manager, the publishing fund which he inaugurated in 1892 was used to support this work.

The Lyceum Movement with its own Manual and Songster spread all over the country, children flocked to the Lyceums, the Union grew in strength and the members were all presented with badges engraved with the photograph of the original founder, A. J. Davis.

In 1910, the Sheffield Education Scheme was launched and it was decided to form a National Scheme but it was not until 1915 that the British Spiritualists Lyceum Union appointed a committee of education and a syllabus was compiled, resulting in Lyceumists being examined according to the set syllabus. London followed the idea and a similar scheme was started in 1916. However, in 1926, both the Sheffield and the London Education Committees were amalgamated and linked up with the Spiritualists National Union Education Scheme, forming together the National Spiritualist College in 1926, but this was closed in 1938.

After several attempts to unite the Spiritualists National Union and the British Spiritualists Lyceum Union, it eventually came to agreement and the two were incorporated (the latter becoming the "Lyceum Department of the S.N.U.") as from June, 1948.

According to the statement of A. J. Davis at Dodworth's Hall, Summerland is divided into different districts with such names as Crystal Lake, Rock Nook,

Happy Valley, etc. It is taught that little children who have passed into the spirit world after a long illness are taken to Crystal Lake to recuperate. Such is the nonsense that is put into the minds of children attending Lyceum meetings.

Spirit children are supposed to have their own instructors and games. They are taught how to return to earth to give messages, and are given to understand that they have no time to quarrel or to be discontented, because they are always busy and happy.

The Lyceum, although it meets on Sunday, is most unlike an ordinary Sunday School, the object being, as described by the London District Lyceum Manual, to instill into children at the earliest age, the knowledge that they are "immortal spirits." There is no mention of the Lord Jesus Christ as a dying Saviour making atonement for sins; it is taught that the object of meeting together is to help one another to study, not the Word of God, but life in the Summerland, which A. J. Davis maintained was a revelation sent to him from God. The greater part of the Lyceum meeting is taken up with discussion. Officers are elected yearly by the members themselves from the age of 12 years and upwards. The Superintendent (or Conductor) has to see that the children get the greatest benefit from each lesson while other officers, such as the Musical Conductor, Guardian of the groups, etc., have their duties to ensure the easy running of the work.

A. J. Davis introduced twelve groups, which were regarded as standards, according to age and progress of the students. They indicate what he considered to be a steady progress and advancement resulting in the growth of the children in wisdom and stature and spiritual maturity. The groups are as follows:—

(1) Fountain group: the beginning of progress.

(2) A Stream group: flowing on from the mountain.

(3) A River group: flowing from the stream.

(4) A Lake group: composed of elements from the river.

(5) The Sea group: growing from the lake.

(6) The Ocean group: swallowing up the sea components. When the child has reached the 6th standard, they are supposed to see "The Beacon (7th standard)"; on the "Shore (8)"; next, waving in the fresh air is seen "A Banner of Progress (9th)"; after which they must look above and discover "A New Star (10th)"; this is followed by what is regarded as "An Aspiring Excelsior" which is supposed to enter the heart. Finally, after passing from the Fountain group to the Excelsior stage, they enter the last class (12th standard) "Liberty," which is the final stage. During all this time, of course, no mention is made of the fall of man or the blood of the Lord Jesus Christ, shed from the remission of sins.

The Lyceum Manual is used at every meeting, and additionally there is what is referred to as "the usual religious exercise". This can be writings by any religious thinker—Christian or otherwise—such as Buddha, Confucius, etc., as it is maintained by the teachers that a good quotation of any individual can be used for the benefit of mankind. These writings are read and meditated upon. After this follows "The Silver Chain" which is a short poem where the Conductor reads one verse and the children read the next. The poems make no mention of a personal salvation. Then comes a musical reading which is usually a hymn with reading between each verse, followed by what is termed the Golden Chain, which is a series of paragraphs or sentences read by the Conductor, one of which is discussed more fully. Taking the two chains independently, the Silver Chain teaches moral lessons, the Golden Chain deals with such subjects as spiritual gifts, Brotherhood, Truth and teachings of Spiritualism, etc.

The Golden Chain is followed in most Lyceums by marching and calisthenics (exercises calculated to increase gracefulness of body). These marches are purporting to be similar to marches performed by the spirit children and have a psychic meaning. After the marching and calisthenics, the Lyceumists go into their different groups for class and the Lyceum eventually closes with a hymn and benediction.

The Golden Chain is followed in most Lyceums by sending their own children to these meetings and not to an ordinary Sunday School and they claim that if a child from its early years learns that intercourse with the dead is possible, it will grow up certain of the fact and be a useful member of the Spiritualist movement. They make every endeavor to advertise the Lyceum by instructing the members to tell other children and get them to come to the meetings, impressing them to repeat all they have learned at the Lyceum to their parents so that they also may take an interest in Spiritualism, if they are not already interested.

Every encouragement is given to children to join, and it is sad to say that this system of teaching is rapidly spreading in the Movement both in England and abroad. The teachers are trained and passed by their own Education Committee, being well-versed in the Lyceum Manual upon which the whole of the erroneous system of teaching is based.

The challenge of Spiritualism, having presented itself to the Sunday Schools of our churches, where the gospel is preached, warns us that the time cannot be wasted which is at our disposal to teach the young the ways of true salvation. We must get the truth of the glorious gospel of salvation into their hearts and minds, so that they may gain a true knowledge of the saving power of the Lord Jesus. We can indeed rejoice when we see children becoming new creatures in Christ and even in addition when we see them receiving the baptism in the Holy Ghost, being equipped for the service of the Lord with power to overcome such subtile deception by Satan and his misguided followers. It is our duty to see that we "train up a child in the way he should go, and when he is old, he will not depart from it" (Proverbs 22:6).

CHAPTER VI

THE DEVELOPING CIRCLE

*". . . and there appeared unto them cloven tongues like as of
fire, and it sat upon each of them, and they were all filled
with the Holy Ghost and began to speak with other tongues
as the Spirit gave them utterance."*

ACTS 2:3 & 4

*". . . to another divers kinds of tongues; to another the in-
terpretation of tongues."*

I COR. 12:10

WHEN Satan has gained a new convert to Spiritualism
his next step is to feed the "new born child" on the
milk of his own lies and, following the scriptural in-
junction to assemble together (thus avoiding any sus-
picion on the part of the new believer), the convert
will find that he will be received with a warm wel-
come and will have the desire to go deeper into the
newly found religion. He will make many mistakes to
start with, like many converts to Christ, who start off
full of zeal, thinking they are going to convert the
whole world, until they realize the necessity of waiting
upon the Lord for direction. The new convert to Spirit-
ualism is very much the same and has to learn to wait
upon the "leadings" of the spirits—the best way to ob-
tain these leadings is by sitting in a developing circle.
This is a circle (group of people) for those who wish

to learn how to develop their psychic gifts and where proper instruction can be obtained from one who understands the methods of the spirits.

Most Spiritualist churches run a Developing Circle for the benefit of newcomers and many of these circles are also run in private homes. In both cases they are managed by an experienced medium who is capable of keeping order in case any "mischievous" or "evil" spirit needs dealing with. It is generally taught that there are some spirits who are "earth-bound," mainly because they are supposed to have died suddenly, being unaware of the fact that they are "dead" and no longer in their physical body, and are therefore unaccustomed to their surroundings. This type of spirit will be dealt with in Chapter 10.

The Developing Circle is very often conducted with a red or blue light, so that the sitters may be in a restful position and condition. Some, however, are held in ordinary light, contrary to the belief that seances are held in darkness all the time, as so many seem to believe. The circle may last for as long as two hours while quiet music is played on a phonograph and the only person moving about in the circle is the leader (the medium in charge) to advise and assist beginners. The sitters are told to concentrate on higher things—to think of making a contact with the other world and to see that their sitting position is comfortable. Relaxation is the order, and care must be taken not to cross the legs as this is supposed to break contact with the spirits. Sitters may be told to hold hands in order that the power may be circulated evenly, although it does not necessarily follow that hands are held in every circle.

The circle progresses quietly and peaceably, the sitters trying to forget themselves mentally and physically, allowing any kind of thought to enter the mind, which according to teaching, is, in all probability, a message from the spirit world. The sitter, having arrived at a state of passivity is just in the position required for evil spirits to work through him. The individual thinks this working is of God and is therefore deceived into believing anything that is taught by the demon who is impersonating the spirit of the dead.

After a time the leader of the circle calls everyone to order and first one and then another is encouraged to relate experiences obtained, while the circle was in progress, until everyone has spoken. They will then be allowed to say whether anything strange was seen in connection with the other sitters in the circle. As a medium who has taken charge of many developing circles, I can say that I heard fantastic things which could easily have been put down as just plain imagination, and students have to learn to discriminate between what is really "spirit" and what may be just a touch of migraine. Teaching is given not to accept everything that comes to one, but to test all things and see that they are correct. By giving out all things that come into their minds would-be mediums learn how to receive and to give, as it is taught again that the more one gives out, the more one will receive. Although only a small percentage of things at the beginning is actually attributable to the supernatural, it is the teacher's place to explain the various reactions, teaching how to differentiate between an "evil" spirit and a "good" spirit. As will be seen in Chapter 10, Spiritualists regard some spirits as "evil" and some as "good," whereas, of course, from a scriptural point of view, all are bad.

It is possible that there may be several sittings before anything constructive takes place, mainly because the student is probably shy of saying something that may sound trivial. In any case the student is learning to relax his body and to keep his mind on one thing until he has reached a state of what could be regarded as self-hypnosis and passivity, which results in his not thinking for himself. He becomes an automaton through which evil spirits work by taking advantage of his passivity. This is, emphatically, not the way the Holy Ghost works, seeing that the Lord does not take away our powers of thinking or conscious action following our thoughts.

Having listened to the thoughts and experiences of the sitters and tried to explain them as best as he can, the leader will then tell the students of what he himself has seen, heard or felt, from the spirit world; description of various spirit forms which can only be seen clairvoyantly (clairvoyance is the power to *see* spirits not visible to everyone) and anything about the sitters which he has observed during the progress of the circle. He would describe "spirit guides" to some, and these would take the form of Indians, Egyptians, Africans, Nuns and Priests, etc.

In time almost every medium gets to know his "guides". There may be several guides for different purposes; for instance, I had a spirit guide who claimed to be an African Witch Doctor, stating that he had been in the spirit world for 600 years and declaring himself to be my "door-keeper" to keep out evil spirits from my body. (I realize just how much of a door-keeper he was when this familiar spirit attempted to kill me when it became obvious that I was out to denounce Spiritualism.) This guide, however, stated that while on earth he used to eat white people and this resulted in his being taken prisoner by white folk, tortured, blinded and put to death. He was, nevertheless, only anxious to come back to earth to do good, actuated by a feeling of forgiveness and repentance for past deeds. Much work was done by this spirit—healing and other types of phenomena—and he also co-operated with other spirits who claimed to be working for the good of mankind. Among these co-workers was another that worked very closely with the witch-doctor, and between them produced the "direct voice" and "materialization" phenomena while I was in deep trance, unconscious of what was going on.

Having been introduced to his guides the beginner realizes that he is developing into a medium, which is what every Spiritualist wants to be. He is encouraged with the thoughts of guides and now has a greater incentive to go deeper (just where the enemy of his soul wants him to go, deeper into the pit of destruction). He is now taking matters more seriously than ever and goes all out for psychic development. It may be some time before he is actually controlled by his guide, but he continues to sit and wait for something to happen. I was considered very fortunate by other envious students when I went into deep trance and was controlled by my African guide, at my first sitting in a developing circle. A man sitting in that same circle who also understood the African dialect conversed quite naturally with the spirit who was controlling me and interpreted what was being said into English. I myself have never known a word of any African dialect. The reader must make no mistake about it, this spirit power is real and not just mere hallucination. Satan is alive and because he is a defeated foe, and *knows* it, he is working to the uttermost to destroy the Church of Christ while he still has the time at his disposal.

The would-be medium, after being encouraged by

the teacher and messages received from the spirits through either the teacher or other sitters, is able to experience what they consider to be identical with the baptism of the Holy Ghost, that is to say, the spirit guide taking control of the body. A spirit guide is a spirit that is more or less constantly in attendance on the medium (or would-be medium, as all people are supposed to have spirit guides, whether they ever become conscious of their present guiding or not). The guide watches over his particular medium and is the first spirit to take control of the body or mind—hence he becomes a "familiar" spirit, giving guidance and advice to the medium. When other spirits wish to use the medium to pass on messages, the guide either introduces the new spirits to the assembled company or else merely describes them and passes on their message. Spirit control takes different forms and is referred to as "Light control" and Trance.

In the case of light control, there is little if any difference about the medium or his voice, although it becomes obvious that whoever is doing the speaking it is not the medium himself. The latter is fully conscious of what is going on in the circle and also is aware of what he is saying. He has, however, no control over his words, his lips being under the sway of the "spirit" and his mind being subordinate to the powers of darkness. The controlling spirit invariably delivers a long address full of deep truths and great wisdom, and will give its name and nationality (i.e., what country it belonged to when alive in a body) and explain what it wants the medium to do. It may describe other types of phenomena. For physical mediumship, however, as against mental mediumship, the medium usually goes into trance.

This goes deeper than light control—it is a term

used very loosely in popular speech to denote any kind of sleep state that presents differences to the normal sleep of a person. When a medium is about to go into trance, he will begin to breathe deeply and heavily and it is a theory among some Spiritualists that the medium's own spirit leaves his body, the controlling spirit taking its place. By this theory, the medium's own spirit is taken to other realms in the spirit world which he is completely unable to describe on his return to earth apart from a general impression that it is full of brightness. Trance mediumship has various stages of development but more will be said about that in due course.

During the process of the medium's spirit leaving the body (we will refer to this theory since it is more or less fitting to resulting facts, for the sake of clarity) the medium will breathe heavily, but will suddenly stop breathing altogether until the spirit guide enters the body to speak, which is a matter of split seconds from the time one stops breathing. The medium's body becomes cold to the touch, as if dead, and when the spirit speaks, it uses the vocal organs of the body which it is possessing. The voice of the medium definitely changes into the recognizable accents of the spirit guide—recognizable, that is, after a little acquaintance with the guide. The medium himself is not conscious of anything that is being said or done. The other sitters sense the spirit's presence either by cool breezes which seem to spread around the room or by heat permeating likewise. The latter invariably signifies that the guide is a healing guide.

Although trance is used for different forms of physical phenomena, a more advanced state is "deep trance". This is the same as ordinary trance but intensified to a much greater degree and leaves the medium feeling completely exhausted, rather as if one has just recovered from a severe illness leaving one weak to the point of trembling, after the departure of the controlling spirit, which process is the same as its entrance to the body, only in reverse.

During this deep trance the medium's actual body has been used to produce physical phenomena and strength has been drawn from it, which is naturally more weakening than having one's mind and lips controlled only. During this process of entering and departing from the medium's body, the spirit demands absolute silence on the part of the sitters, as a sudden noise, movement, etc., may result in the medium receiving a violent shock to his system and may even go so far as to cause him to lose his life. Mediumship then is certainly not a thing to tamper with unless one is prepared to risk everything for it. Again, during deep trance, the medium's own spirit travels through realms of light, but at my last seance this was reversed for me, and all I could recall upon regaining consciousness was that for once I had been travelling through realms of darkness and the spirits were trying to take away my life by preventing me returning to my body. It seemed as if some superhuman effort, which came from somewhere outside of myself, succeeded in gaining the victory and I managed to return to my body. Since this was my last seance, and my thoughts previous to it had been more on Isaiah 53 and my newly awakened interest in the Lord Jesus Christ than they were on the seance and my guides, I believe that the Lord was there to deliver me that night and won a victory over the powers of darkness for me that I could never have won for myself. Truly He doeth all things well! If the Enemy had succeeded in taking my life, this testimony to the saving power of the Christ of

God would never have been written, and this was possibly the thought behind the attack—to snatch one more away into destruction before a decision could be made for Christ.

Frequently in the course of development students will see many colored lights, all of which are presumed to denote different things, such as healing, purity, love, etc.; and when a medium is about to enter into trance, these spirit lights can often be seen just before the guide is due to take control. Also when the guide does enter and speak, he is invariably a native of a different country (or had been when on earth) from the medium's own and speaks in the language of the nation he states he belongs to. This foreign language is often interpreted into the language of those present in the circle by another spirit guide who is controlling the body of another person in the circle simultaneously. This speaking and interpretation is Satan's counterfeit of the Baptism of the Holy Ghost and the gifts of tongues and interpretation of tongues.

Spiritualists claim that these conditions are identical with the Pentecostal experience of Acts 2, and the Devil has even given them spirit lights to imitate the cloven tongues of fire. Here and there, there are actually Spiritualist churches professing to be "Pentecostal" and the name is naturally misleading to a lot of Christians. I can give personal testimony to the mighty difference between the Spiritualists' baptism (i.e., spirit control) and the baptism of the Holy Ghost, having experienced both.

Mr. M. F. Bovenizer, a one-time Methodist Minister, who stated that he was bundled out of the Methodist Ministry because he could not reconcile the love of God with the Church's doctrine of Hell (which he refused to teach) and eventually became a Christian

Spiritualist, states regarding the Pentecostal experience:

"The morning of Pentecost found about 120 gathered in the Upper Room waiting for the fulfilment of the Master's promise, when suddenly the rushing sound as of a mighty wind ended their suspense. The indoor storm filled the room where they were sitting. It was accompanied by the appearance of what we call spirit lights in the shape of tongues which floated or hovered above the heads of the sitters."

Note that he remarks ". . . what *we* call spirit lights . . ." referring to the sign mentioned above. He continues:

"These phenomena accompanied the invasion of the Upper Room by a host of spirits from high spheres, who forthwith overshadowed and took possession of the assembled mortals."

Note again that when Jesus promised the Comforter, which is the Holy Ghost, He referred to the Holy Spirit and not spirits (plural). The ex-parson continues:

"Literally these spirits clothed themselves with the bodies of those present in the Upper Room, just as it happened with Gideon in the Old Testament record."

(Judges 6:34.)

Note that this verse in Judges refers again to the Spirit of the Lord and not a spirit. Mr. Bovenizer goes on to say that these spirits began to speak through the mouths of the members of the assembly and *the same process and operation takes place* in the case of trance control during seances today.

Later on he writes:

"These experiences definitely indicate that the faith which led to the founding of the Christian Church on the day of Pentecost was a Spiritualist and demonstrable faith, in contrast to the faith of our modern days, so frequently described as blind belief."

The same writer tells us that he was privileged to witness these same things in an unforgettable form during the early stages of the Welsh Revival, and he kindly tells us that the Pentecostal Community of Churches still possess the gifts of prophecy and tongues that functioned during the Welsh Revival, but that these gifts are exercised by their holders, in total oblivion of their relations to psychic powers! Once more I can add personal testimony and say that the gifts given by the Holy Spirit are wonderfully different from those given by demons—having once more experienced both!

It is very obvious that Satan is using an extremely subtle counterfeit to the precious gifts of the Spirit and this should cause the Christian to seek the power of this baptism of the Holy Ghost and not be satisfied until he receives it, with the initial evidence of the speaking in other tongues as the Spirit gives utterance. It does not need much thought to realize that if the Devil has a counterfeit of the Baptism of the Holy Ghost and the gifts of the Spirit, it must be the will of the Lord that all His children should be filled with the real Spirit and God-given power, exercising the actual spiritual gifts and thus prepared to live an overcoming, supernatural life in Christ. Otherwise, there would be no point in the Devil going to such lengths to create a counterfeit, as it would be no lure to the unwary.

It is because Satan knows that the Christian life should be demonstrable—as Mr. Bovenizer puts it—and as the Scriptures also put it . . . "these signs shall follow them that believe . . ." (Mark 16:17), that he takes the demonstrable part and counterfeits it. Something that can be seen and felt, that is tangible, is easier believed in than something that is not—and many people really seeking a satisfying knowledge of God are drawn into Spiritualism by these very signs, which gives them something to take hold of.

Only the real power of God working through His people, through His Spirit, will reveal the second-best efforts of Satan in this direction and will clear the darkened minds of his dupes. Praise God, He can see our hearts and the desires of those who wish to know the truth and although there may be many tossings about during the search . . . His promise is that those that seek Him, shall find Him, Whom to know is life eternal. Unfortunately, many are misled into thinking they have the truth in Spiritualism and so give up the real search for the Lord and so they do not find Him. Let us pray that Light shall be shed in dark places and they shall be led to know good from evil.

CHAPTER VII

CLAIRVOYANCE AND CLAIRAUDIENCE

"... to another, the discerning of spirits ..."
                                        I COR. 12:10.

"... and thine ears shall hear a word behind thee."
                                        ISAIAH 30:21.

MEDIUMSHIP falls into sections, Mental mediumship
and Physical mediumship. The most common form of
mental mediumship is clairvoyance and clairaudience,
which is the power to see and to hear clearly—the
former covering the ability to see supernatural things,
the latter covering the hearing of them.

This gift, as practiced by Spiritualist mediums, is
mistaken for the supernatural gift of the Spirit re-
ferred to as "discerning of spirits" which is also the
power to recognize the origin of supernatural things.
It must constantly be remembered that there is a true
as well as a false recognition of supernatural manifes-
tations and, therefore, this gift can either be a Divine
gift which is the true manifestation of God, or the re-
sult of a passive state expected of a medium who is
"developing" or has "developed".

Spiritualists claim that the gift of clairvoyance and
clairaudience is one gift; that it is a natural one that
exists in everyone and it only requires developing and

instruction to be properly exercised. We consider the exercise of it to be the result of demon control and inspiration, its *modus operandi* being entirely different from the Divine gift of revelation which leaves the mental faculties untouched and undisturbed. It is well to remember that the people around Mount Sinai were not in a "passive" state, but mentally alert when they saw the manifestation of God, neither were the disciples on the Mount of Transfiguration when they saw Moses and Elias, nor were they "tuned in" to the spirit world, being perfectly natural at the time, not apparently even thinking of such manifestations.

This type of mediumship is very often referred to as thought reading or the ability to be able to tell a person of his faults and shortcomings, but it is not so. Mediums are not trained as thought readers and being able to tell the character of people does not enter into it. It is purely and simply what it says it is, the discerning of spirits and it is spirits which they actually see. Satan has very cleverly imitated this gift of the Spirit, producing his own in contrast to the Divine manifestation in the true Church.

On close examination of the counterfeit gift, we shall see how demons not only use the same methods as the Holy Spirit, but the gift is used for the same purpose!

Visions which are divine and seen by a child of God who is endowed with this supernatural gift, mentioned in I Cor. 12:10, usually have definite results. If however, we watch the counterfeit as we see it in Spiritualism, we will find that it invariably results in nothing but intangibility. Although the spirits utter great words of truth, suggestions of perversion are carefully intermingled, and result in the denial of the necessity of either regeneration or the building up of the spiritual side of the believer.

The powers of darkness are not afraid of words of truth, the gospel, or the mention of the Blood of Jesus, if there is no power behind the words. They are even prepared to allow some of the gospel truths to be taught, providing there is no real conviction behind the actual teaching. I was once told by a Christian that one would only have to walk into a Spiritualists' meeting with a Bible in one's pocket and the meeting would be broken up. He was very surprised when I told him that I always used to carry a Bible in my pocket when I was a Spiritualist but it did not stop any phenomena occurring! It is also a fairly current belief that one only has to mention the Blood of Jesus and any Spiritualist would walk out of a meeting. Let us not be deceived into a lackadaisical way of applying the Blood of Jesus to fit in with our own requirements. The mentioning of the Blood has become such a habit in some churches that people have come to think it can be used in every conceivable manner. One Christian refused to lock his windows as a precaution against burglars saying that "his house was under the Blood." This cannot be so as nothing is under the Blood except our sins. "Blessed are they whose sins are covered." (Romans 4, 7.) We read that one overcomes by the "power" of the Blood, not by the covering of the Blood. Nevertheless it has become a point among a good many Christian assemblies to pray for a covering of the Blood upon their meetings and actions, rather than to seek to overcome by the power of the Blood. Consequently many thinking and praying in this fashion are easily deceived into considering that any manifestation that takes place is obviously from God because they prayed for a "covering." This gives Satan an opportunity to step in with cunning deceptions. It should also be remembered that in Exodus 12 we read that at the Passover the children of Israel were to "sprinkle" the blood on their door posts, and there is again no mention of "covering by" the Blood. We should take the lesson from the Passover incident that is implied and be sure that the Blood is being continually sprinkled or applied to our hearts and to be ever mindful that when we do fall and stumble in the Christian Way, that "the Blood of Jesus Christ cleanses us from all sin." Some little time ago I was addressing a Church with a mixed congregation of Christians and Spiritualists, and they all joined in singing the hymn, "What can wash away my sin, nothing but the blood of Jesus." No one walked out, which is just as well, as I should not have been able to preach against Spiritualism which was what I was there for. It did happen that towards the end of the meeting three of the Spiritualists walked out shouting, "Why have you come to upset us?" and "Why don't you leave us alone?" This was no doubt because of the power of the Blood in the Word that was being preached, faithfully, I trust, and not because the meeting was "covered" by the Blood. Certainly the meeting was infused with the power of the Holy Ghost and the prayers of the saints trusting in the power of the Blood to overcome resulted in the Lord being mightily victorious. The Devil does not mind in the least how much we mention the blood provided it is not done under the power of the Holy Spirit. Thus a child of God, not equipped with the supernatural power of the Holy Ghost, together with a knowledge of the Word of God (which is the sword of the Spirit) rightly divided, is likely to be deceived into believing that the Spiritualist movement, doing such "good" works, must be of God. The powers of darkness would indeed tremble at the Word of Truth, preached under the anointing of the Holy Ghost, spoken as the oracles of God and not of man. It is the duty of every born-again child of God to claim this enduement of power and seek the baptism of the Holy Ghost and so be equipped to battle against the supernatural powers of darkness.

The manifestations of clairvoyance and clairaudience usually work together and are regarded, as I said before, as one gift. It has been known, however, for a medium to possess either one or the other separately, in which case it is generally developed to a marked degree.

It is possible for the medium to give a demonstration of this gift at any seance or public meeting, in a bus, train, restaurant or park. It does not require any special lighting and can be demonstrated anywhere. No form of trance condition is necessary, only the tuning in to the spirit world by the medium, who being in a passive state of mind is open to receive messages from those who presume to be the spirits of the dead.

Recognition of the spirits by the audience depends entirely upon the descriptions given by the medium who has, therefore, to learn the art of being able to give a clear description and has to be trusted to give the message properly from the spirit to the listener—who cannot see or hear anything of the spirits for themselves—so that we see that with the exercise of this gift the listener has to trust the medium. The Word of God, however, has taught us the all-important lesson in His Word, "Thus saith the Lord, cursed be the man that trusteth in man and maketh flesh his arm and whose heart departeth from the Lord" (Jer. 17:5), and again, "Blessed is the man that trusteth in the Lord and whose hope the Lord is" (Jer. 17:7).

Some mediums have this gift only to a slight degree and instead of actually seeing the spirits themselves, see only signs and symbols, the meaning of which the sitter has to fathom out for himself. I remember an occasion at a fairly large public meeting when the demonstrating medium was one of the "sign and symbol" type, and after giving several messages which meant one thing or another to the receivers, she pointed to a lady sitting at the back of the hall and told her that above her head she could see a mustard tin in spirit form! The lady in question had not the faintest idea of the meaning of this and so, no doubt hoped that the medium would find that it had a connection with someone else. The medium, however, was not going to be put off as easily as all that and insisted that the spirit form of the unwanted mustard tin was still reposing lovingly upon the head of the woman. A deadlock seemed imminent, with the woman emphatically disclaiming any connection with the mustard tin and the medium being just as insistent that the lonely tin belonged to the woman, while the mustard tin itself was apparently also as certain that it was not going to budge until someone claimed it. The medium eventually eased the situation by saying, "Well, madam, whether you like it or not, the mustard tin belongs to you and if you will give time for thought you will realize why." After a slight pause, during which time the woman duly gave a very little time for thought, she replied, "Well, the only reason why I can think of you seeing a mustard tin above my head is because my name is Coleman," apparently linking the mustard tin with a certain brand of this part of the household spice shelf. Presumably this was the correct reason in spite of its triviality, for the tin, no doubt satisfied with the wonderful evidence it had given of survival, returned back to the spirit world. Did it go to the spirits' food stores to be replenished with mustard to warm the spirits up when they sit down to dinner during a cold winter's day? The Lord is preparing a hot place for these impersonating demons where they will not need mustard!

The above incident brought a touch of hilarity to the meeting, but it can be said that most good demonstrators of this satanic gift usually aspire to better evidence than that, and those who desire more evidential visions find that the devil obligingly gives them when he sees that mediums are prepared to make sacrifices and go all out to further develop the gift. There are many mediums who are able to describe these supposed spirits of the dead to a most remarkable degree, giving evidence that is very satisfying to enquirers. The reader should reserve no doubts about the fact that these mediums can and do see spirits. They would not be able to claim this gift to be the actual gift of the Spirit if this were not so. The child of God knows that it is not possible for one to return from the dead and therefore realizes that it must be demons impersonating the spirits of the dead, but the medium and the average enquirer are equally deceived into believing that such contact is wrought by the hand of God.

After discovering the owner of the spirit who is said to be trying to make contact, the medium will then proceed to tell the recipient of anything the spirit wants to say. Only the medium can see the spirit, unless others in the congregation also have the gift and happened to be tuned in to the same "vibration." The medium will then endeavor to prove that the spirit is actually the dead relative as it states itself to be, as the possibility is allowed by the medium that the spirit may be a bad spirit trying to fool about and every safeguard has to be taken. The communicating spirit invariably gives all the required proof quite easily by mentioning intimate things that the enquirer may not know himself, but which later prove to be true. Sometimes the communicating spirit will pretend to be an evil spirit by making deliberate mistakes and this gives a good excuse for adherents of this cult when anything goes wrong to put it down to the agency of evil spirits, confusing the contacts.

It may occur to the reader to wonder why, if the communicating spirits are impersonating demons and not the spirits of departed relatives of the enquirer (which most of them give evidence of being) they are able to give intimate details of their lives upon earth and likewise of the habits, etc., of the enquirer? Is it possible for the spirits to thought-read the enquirer while in the seance or have they intimate knowledge of their lives already gained before the sitting? It is not, of course, possible to give a comprehensive answer to this as we are not aware of everything that goes on in the atmosphere around us. We can only understand as far as revelation has been granted us from the Word of God, and from experiences in the past. From observation, and from various statements made by these communicating spirits, it is reasonable to conclude that they both read the thoughts of the enquirer and have also become familiar with the enquirer's life and background. Communicating spirits often imply that they can impress the mind of a person with *their* thoughts, which can be done so naturally that the person believes them to be his own thoughts. Their own teaching of "guides" that constantly watch over people, being attracted to a particular person by a similarity of interests and characteristic traits, implies that they must be aware of our actions and thoughts, other-

wise they would be in no position to presume to guide.
We can discount their motives for such close watch-
ing, which they say is for the benefit of humanity, to
lead us to truth and happiness, but we have no reason
to suppose that it is impossible that demons should be
capable of watching us in this way. The very facts
which they do reveal during seances are fairly strong
evidence of an exceedingly close watch since minute
details are given in most instances. On the other hand,
during some methods of communication, those of
clairvoyance and clairaudience as we have just been
discussing, evidence is given that shows that commu-
nicating spirits can also thought-read. For example,
the medium gives a message to someone in the audi-
ence or circle, purporting to be from a departed friend
or relative. As proof of the identity of this communi-
cating spirit, the person in the audience is told that the
spirit saw this person standing underneath a large pic-
ture, holding a watch in his hand (the time shown on
the watch is given) and the person was *thinking* of a
particular experience that had happened to him. The
person thus addressed will, almost without exception,
admit to having stood in the position described, at the
time mentioned, and to have been thinking about the
experience mentioned. There are many instances simi-
lar to this which do go to prove that it is possible for
the spirits to thought-read. One spirit is recorded to
have said that "she could see right into the mind of the
person she was talking to" during a seance, and we
have no real reason for doubting this. Again, however,
there are times when particulars and incidents are dis-
closed to enquirers that are completely unknown by
them at the time and have to be checked up on after-
wards. Again, almost invariably, the information given
proves to be correct, which rules out the possibility

that all the information given through mediums is merely a matter of thought-reading. It implies that thought-reading is only one of the means employed by the demons to draw an enquirer into a believing frame of mind. It is this uncanny knowledge of past and present events and activities that convinces so many people that they are literally communicating with departed relatives and friends and guides. Naturally this knowledge is one of the most effective weapons in the armory of the hosts of darkness and will be wielded by them to its fullest extent, and the demons themselves will see to it that their knowledge of us is perfected in every way possible, and used with the utmost skill and exactitude to accomplish their purpose. The exactitude of their knowledge, by the way, is not entirely absolute—they do slip up on minor points of detail, e.g., in the instance quoted above, the person holding the watch may have been said to be holding a *gold watch*, whereas in actuality it was a *silver* watch. This does not materially affect the evidence given, and in any case is usually accounted for by Spiritualists as either showing the human element to be still existent in the communicating spirit (their fallibility) or else it lies in a faulty communication between spirit and medium. We might take it, from our point of view, that the espionage service of the demon powers has not been so meticulous in its operation as it usually is, but nevertheless, these minor details do not detract from the weight of "evidence" given to the enquirer, which is usually sufficiently accurate to inspire belief.

The Word of God implies that these spirits (demons) are legion, so there is no difficulty in conceiving that there are sufficient of them to be able to investigate pretty thoroughly into the lives of everyone, and we have no knowledge of the capacity of their intelligences. Their scope for activity must necessarily be much wider than ours. We must remember too that these demons are under the leadership and direction of Satan himself—a very much under-rated being, by most of us—but whom the Scriptures reveal as an extremely powerful intelligence, ever-warring against mankind, attempting to deceive men in all ways, thus leading them away from God. References are made also to his princes and hosts of wicked spirits carrying out his will—all of which amounts to the fact that his forces are certainly numerous and powerful enough to encompass his design to deceive the whole world. The forces of evil, as revealed in the Book of Revelation, are most definitely capable of hoodwinking human beings, if we are not effectively alert for such operations. Although Satan is the father of lies, he is not averse to using half-truths and is an adept in wielding even the truth itself when it can be twisted to the ruination of man, as we see from many instances in the Word of God. Let us as Christians ever be conscious of the fact that we are warring against principalities and powers, rulers of the darkness of this world, against spiritual wickedness in high places, but let us also remember that greater is He that is in us, than he that is in the world. Amen.

CHAPTER VIII

PSYCHOMETRY

"... to one is given by the Spirit the word of wisdom, to
another the word of knowledge by the same spirit."

I Cor. 12:8.

"... to another prophecy. ..."

I Cor. 12:10.

CONTINUING "mental" mediumship, which includes
psychometry—this usually runs co-operatively with
those gifts already mentioned of clairvoyance and
clairaudience, as it is possible to demonstrate psychom-
etry under the same conditions, e.g., in public halls,
parks, seances, etc. *It is regarded as the power to
make a personal contact with a live person or persons
who are absent from the place where it is being dem-
onstrated, and also to make contact with the spirits of
the dead,* through being able to *handle an article*
which belongs or belonged either to the dead person
or to the absent one.

At certain times special meetings are held in Spiritu-
alist churches when a medium will give a demon-
stration of psychometry. Although regarded as one of
the more common types of mediumship, it usually
draws many people who are anxious for a message of
advice from the spirits. It can be developed to a very

high standard, according, of course, to the willingness of the medium to forsake everything else and concentrate on obtaining good results.

Psychometry meetings vary in size. People attending usually place an article, belonging either to themselves or a lost relative, on a tray and then sit down with others also anxious to receive some message of comfort or advice. One after another will enter the room and carefully place his article on the tray, taking great care not to touch anyone else's article for fear of interfering with the etheric vibrations and thus spoiling someone's "message." When all the company is ready the medium, being ignorant of the owners of each individual article, will take one up at random and begin to relate the thoughts or feelings which come to him while holding the article. The article is presumed to be making contact with the enquirer and through this means the medium, with the aid of the communicating spirits, is able to relate many things regarding the owner's condition of mind and life. Care will be taken in giving out secrets that may be precious or embarrassing, and tactful terms are used that can be understood by the enquirer and no one else. Mediums can usually be trusted to keep any secrets that the spirits reveal to them in private sittings or public meetings and if the matter is very personal, the enquirer may even be asked to remain behind after the meeting to have a private talk with the medium.

Information given is dictated by the spirit guide of the medium and very often, as in other cases, information is given unknown by the enquirer that has to be checked on. Telepathy is out of the question with regard to this gift as is shown in many ways and instances. After the message or information has been given the medium will ask the owner of the article to raise his hand and it will be returned. Quite probably the medium will then see spirits clairvoyantly and will describe them. Further messages are passed on by contact with the articles one by one until all of them have been psychometrised.

This gift was used to a large extent on behalf of anxious parents, wives and relatives during the war years in trying to find the whereabouts of somebody posted as "missing." Messages of hope were given to many which proved to be true, although it is also a fact that the spirits have told many lies through the mediums and a lot of people were told that their loved ones were still alive when in actual fact they were dead. This has led to the enquirer anxiously waiting for the return of the "missing" person and haunting Spiritualist meetings in the hope of further news. By the time the lie was discovered, most of them were already habituees of the cult and the lie had served its purpose. Also the thing had gotten such a hold on them that the lie ceased to matter overmuch and certainly did not result in a revulsion of feeling against the whole business, which is what one might expect.

However, most of these messages proved true, as it would not advertise Spiritualism much if lying were excessive. During those war years I can recall an instance where a man brought me an article to psychometrise. With the help of my "guide" I was able to say that the owner of the article was well and was a prisoner-of-war. The article turned out to belong to the man's son. The distracted parent told me I had made a mistake because he had heard that his son had been killed in action and produced the telegram giving this information, which was nearly two weeks old. My guide insisted that the boy was not dead and instructed me to inform the parent that he would receive con-

firmation of this fact within three days. This was
proved absolutely correct when within three days the
man received another telegram informing him that his
son was a prisoner-of-war and well and the previous
telegram was a mistake. Such messages brought many
people to believe that this was the work of God. It
seems fantastic that Satan himself should do many
"good works" with such evil motives as to lead people
away from God. It is obvious that such a power can
only be defeated by those who are filled with the
greater power of the Holy Ghost, because fantastic
though it may sound, we are told with scriptural au-
thority that this is so.

In times past it has been known for mediums to as-
sist the police to trace murderers and thieves from an
article the criminal has left behind at the scene of the
crime, and many criminals have been brought to jus-
tice as a result of the use of this gift. Also mediums
can trace a particular illness through contact with an
article belonging to the sick person and without ever
seeing the invalid, will be able to describe the symp-
toms, diagnose the illness (even in cases where doc-
tors have failed) and prescribe treatment which ends
in the healing of the patient and the surprise of the
doctors.

Psychometry is obviously Satan's counterfeit of the
two gifts of revelation known by Christians as the gift
of wisdom and knowledge and no doubt includes the
other one of prophecy, too. As a result of the exercis-
ing of psychometry people have been warned only just
in time of another's evil intention towards them, their
instant action being able to ward off the intention;
thieves have been discovered, and one's needs have
been met, thoughts have been revealed, the future as
well as the past unveiled—all of which encourages the

enquirer to a firm belief in Spirtualism which can produce such marvels.

Many Spiritualists claim that psychometry is a gift that was practiced by the Lord Jesus Christ and they use John 4 to back up this theory. By their contention, He proved that He could psychometrize because He was able to tell the Samaritan woman all about herself, and again, according to them, He was only able to do this when she handed Him the waterpot with water for Him to drink. The Scriptures, of course, do not mention that she gave Him to drink, but that He merely said "Give me to drink," and from then on we read of the conversation that took place eventually causing the woman to leave her waterpot to tell others that she had found the Messiah. When Spiritualists claim that Jesus was able to tell the woman all about herself, they speak the truth, but the reader will see how very cunningly Satan is able to teach the truth and bring in a lie at the same time. Acquaint a Spiritualist with the fact that the Scriptures do not mention Jesus taking hold of any waterpot in this incident and they will merely say that Jesus could not have told the woman so much *without having done so*. This makes the Lord incapable of revelation with the addition of material things whereas we know that with Him all things are possible. They will also say that, obviously, the Scriptures left out the reference to the waterpot, but we know that had that been of vital importance it would have been included, for therein are written all things necessary to make us wise to salvation. Satan will try every means to bring in lies intermingled with the truth, and this should make every child of God ready to seek after the divine gifts of wisdom and knowledge and prophecy, accepting the fact that God would have these gifts operating in His church today. Satan has the counterfeit—are the children of God to be without the real thing when the Lord says unto us, "Ask and ye shall receive"?

CHAPTER IX

HEALING

"To another the gifts of healing."

I COR. 12:9.

"And they shall lay hands on the sick, and they shall
recover.

MARK 16:18.

THIS is another of the much longed for supernatural
gifts of the Spirit and one desired not only by Chris-
tians, but by Spiritualists also.

This miraculous gift of power is not only exercised
in the true Church of Christ, but also in the false
church. The former is due to the power of the Holy
Spirit, the latter to the operation of what we know as
evil spirits. There are many many Spiritualists today
who are endowed with this remarkable gift of power
by Satan, and I myself, having been used in this way,
can testify to having witnessed miraculous healings
taking place at "healing meetings" in Spiritualism.

Through this type of mediumship the blind have
been made to see, the lame to walk, the deaf to hear,
and it is powerfully drawing folks into the Movement.
It is impossible to doubt the fact that these gifts are in
operation in counterfeit in the Spiritualist movement.
There are different methods for healing the sick in

these meetings and although all Spiritualists do not accept the inspiration of the Bible, they will quote different examples of healings recorded there. They believe in the laying-on of hands according to Mark 16:18 as it works out in practice, and healers have been raised up from time to time who use this method.

Healing meetings are held in large halls from one period of time to another in this country, and all over the land people flock either to see others healed or to receive healing themselves. They can be seen waiting for hours outside the halls before the meeting is due to start, and what a pathetic sight it is to see the sufferers making their way eagerly one by one towards the platform where the healer is waiting. He or she is also anxious to heal the sick and willing to be used to almost any extent to accomplish this purpose.

The healer without asking any questions will lay his "healing hands" on the sufferer and the patient will feel the power being transmitted from the medium to himself. A few moments of silence will reign throughout the whole congregation who will co-operate by concentrating on the patient and sending out "healing thought rays" and "love rays" to assist the medium in his task. Later the one who has sought healing will testify that healing has taken place. Crutches, splints, bath chairs and other appliances left behind prove that the devil has successfully accomplished that which the Church originally set out to do. The person now healed is full of joy and praises of the healer and to the spirits who did the work. Please note that the healing is done by the spirits, the medium is only the vessel through which they work, and everyone, especially the medium himself, is very conscious of this fact. However much the medium may be used, or in whatever way, whether his hands are used for the manipulation of bones, etc., whether he is conscious or unconscious of what is going on, the thanks are returned to the *spirits* who have accomplished the work, in its entirety. The spirits, however, usually modestly ask that their "God" should have the glory—their god incidentally being their father, the Devil, although this is, of course, not plain to Spiritualists.

The healing medium will be physically tired after giving so much healing and through the loss of power which has been given out. It has been recorded that one particular healing medium spent so long giving relief to the sick in a special room set aside for this purpose that he would have to be carried out himself as it left him so weak!

Some healers, before laying on hands, will anoint with oil beforehand (according to the wording of James 5:14) while others do not touch the individual but heal by a word of command.

Up to now we have dealt with healings that can be accomplished in public halls by the laying-on of hands, and anointing with oil and by word of command. These same healings can also be achieved in private home circles so long as a healing medium is present. Such healings take place to the strains of soft music, whether in public hall or private home, either recorded on a phonograph or sung by members of the circle. The medium can be either under light control or in trance according to the type of complaint he is dealing with. For instance, if a person is suffering from an ordinary kind of illness, not of long standing, the medium can anoint with oil, *lay hands* on the sick person and bring about a cure; if the complaint is deeply rooted or of a more serious nature, such as cancer, growths, disfigured limbs, etc., it will probably necessitate *trance for the medium and hypnosis for the patient as* the pain caused by any manipulation or probing would be more than is humanly possible to stand. Hypnosis, therefore, plays an important part in the more difficult cases. Surely God doesn't work in such a manner.

Great success has been achieved in the small home "healing circle" where a healing medium is present, and also results have been fairly common in these circles without a healing medium. As its name implies the sitters in this circle are only interested in healing and at the very commencement of the circle, which can be conducted in ordinary light, special prayers are made for the sick. Names of needy ones are read from the "healing list" and after each name a few minutes silence is maintained during which every member sends out "healing thoughts" to the patient who is absent. When all the names have been read out and if there is time, the whole circle will continue in silence thinking only of healing for the sick. This type of healing is referred to as "Absent Healing" and can be exercised without an actual healing medium in charge. Many bad cases of sickness have been restored to health through this method. It would be just as well if the reader should deviate a little from the Spiritualist "healing circle" and realize how the home prayer meeting is being very carefully and cunningly substituted by the "home healing circle." It is at the home prayer meeting that the testimony of the saints is built up and the family united in one before God. It is a contention among Spiritualists that it is no use just attending public meetings if they are not prepared to develop in their own home circle. Unfortunately there are many children of God who only pray in the public meetings and do not bother overmuch about the home and family prayer meeting.

To return to our subject, this gift of healing is taken by Spiritualists into the open air, as well as to halls and public meetings and home circles. Healings have been effected in streets and parks before crowds of eager bystanders.

Another feature of this is animal healing; Satan has also raised up special mediums who are possessed with this capacity of curing sick animals. We know that John Wesley prayed for his horse and God answered prayer. Considering that God has given us dominion over all animals there does not seem to be anything antiscriptural about asking the Lord to heal a sick beast or household pet. Instances are known where Christians have beseeched Him to lay His hand on a favorite pet and God has answered the earnest prayer of the saints.

Satan naturally wants to cast as much wool over people's eyes as possible and certain spirits teach special methods for the laying of hands upon sick animals. Many Spiritualists testify that their animals have been miraculously restored to health through their mediumship. It is even known that certain of their churches have held actual services for sick animals where people take their pets for the animal healer to heal. It must be born in mind, of course, that Spiritualists believe that animals also progress into the spirit world, so there is nothing incongruous about them being concerned for the welfare of them.

We can see that this gift, like all the other gifts of the spirit, can be either from God or from Satan. The counterfeit must be in appearance as good as the real thing, otherwise it would not fulfill its aim. Many who attend these counterfeit healing meetings become convinced upon seeing these gifts in operation, that God is behind these good works. Some are interested in the works for the works' sake, regardless of what power is behind it. Those who have received healing through Spiritualism are not going to be very easily convinced that it is work of an evil nature.

A young woman recently approached me and said she was extremely distressed to hear me say that the communicating spirits were demons, because they had given her back her sight and surely demons would not do such things. Alas, many think this way and are like this woman once literally blind and now only able to see physical things, being still tragically blind to the things of God. It should grieve the heart of every Christian to realize that Satan is doing the very same good works which the Lord commissioned His disciples to do, while the Church with all the supernatural powers of God at its disposal is neglecting to aspire after the gifts. The neglect of a gift would be a crime to a Spiritualist and in this direction these demon-led, deluded people put us to shame by their zeal and fervor.

Another reason why Satan chooses to counterfeit this gift is that it gives evidence that these spirits have power. This should, of course, be the reason why every child of God should covet earnestly the best gifts, in order to prove that His touch has still its ancient power. Spiritualists go all out to prove the power behind their works by relying entirely on the spirits to work through them. Many of these mediums are ordinary people with only average education, yet they are mightily used by these demons and can diagnose sickness and diseases with an accuracy that has astounded doctors and scientists. We, too, could go all out to prove the power of God by allowing Him to work through us, relying upon Him to the uttermost, keeping ourselves as channels.

Having satisfied the inquirer of the good works and the power of the spirits, they use this gift as a stepping stone towards their main lie "there is no death." The onlooker having seen miracles performed beyond the powers of the ordinary looking mediums used, concludes that the power is "spirit" and Satan's lies have been established once more. If the Word of God were studied instead of heed being given to such blasphemy, it would be found that the followers of this cult are condemned already and are being led very far away from the way of salvation which is through the precious blood of Jesus only, shed on Calvary for sinners. By His stripes we are healed and our iniquities are laid on Him, Who said, "I am the Way, the Truth and the Life, no man cometh unto the Father but by Me."

The Psychic News recently commented on the healing successes of Pastor Howell M. Harris and stated that they applauded his work and commended his efforts, but apparently this Pentecostal pastor was denouncing Spiritualism and Christian Science stating that "if you are in pain, we of the Assemblies of God recognize the fact and tell you of Some One who can deliver you from pain." *The Psychic News* states, "We do not sneer at Pastor Harris' cures, nor do we deny that he is the ideal healer for those to whom his particular approach appeals. Why does he take it upon himself to try to destroy someone else's faith in a different approach?" It is obvious from that statement on behalf of Spiritualism that they give no heed to the fact that Jesus said, "I am the Way," and *Psychic News* continues to prove their opposition to the true church by saying, "Just as there are many roads to God, so also are there many channels through whom spiritual healing is directed to mankind." Their many roads to God are in direct opposition to God's Word and there is no need to print any more of their remarks concerning Pastor Harris. Those poor deluded people may never know the joy of "ten thousand times ten thousand and thousands of thousands; saying with a loud voice, 'Worthy, Worthy is the Lamb that was slain to receive power and riches and wisdom and strength and honor and glory and blessing'." Such will only be possible when we preach the gospel faithfully to those people under the anointing of the Holy Ghost, for how shall they hear without a preacher?

It is possible that converts may be won for Christ through this wonderful gift of healing and God should have the praise for all His love and compassion towards us. The Devil wants this praise to himself and so he uses this very gift counterfeited in order to gain it, using his fallen angels as his tools.

We long to be able to lay hands on the sick and see that they recover, yet we know that it is our own lack of faith and obedience that withholds the demonstrations of God's mighty power to a large extent. He is able, and thank God, He is demonstrating His ability in marvellous ways in many parts of the world, and huge congregations are again coming under the sway of an all-conquering and all-prevailing Saviour, Who is mighty to heal and to save.

CHAPTER X

RESCUE WORK

". . . in My name shall they cast out devils. . . ."
                                        MARK 16:17.

CAN Satan cast out Satan? Can a house divided against itself stand? The answer is emphatically "No," but Satan has carefully devised a method of psychic phenomena which would deceive the very elect, if this were possible—thank God it is not, a scheme which would convince anyone ignorant of the ways of God that Spiritualism "must be of God."

Satan knows that a house divided against itself cannot stand and there is no point in casting out his own demons from a human body, as that would make division. The reader may be surprised to know, however, that *in some Circles there is a literal counterfeit to the casting out of demons.* This chapter is an attempt to show Satan's methods in this direction, that is to say, there is counterfeit of a counterfeit or a copy of a copy, which only one who knows the power of the Holy Ghost and God's Word can really understand. Spirit-filled believers know that Jesus said, *"In My Name* shall they cast out demons," but demons blind the Spiritualist into ignoring the source of the real power to cast out demons which is based solely upon "His Name." Any other name is powerless and even the use of the Lord's Name is of no avail without the power behind the command to "come out." In Acts 19 we read of the vagabond Jews, exorcists who tried to cast out evil spirits saying, "We adjure you by Jesus whom Paul preacheth," and the answer of the evil spirit saying, "Jesus I know, and Paul I know, but who are ye?" The man then leaped on them and overcame them! They thought that just the mention of the Name of Jesus would be sufficient but obviously this is not so.

Satan cleverly twists Scripture round to make his followers believe that he is non-existent and that there are no such things as fallen angels. No devil, No fallen angels, No hell; This puts him in an awkward position if he wants to make his followers believe that they are doing God's work, so *he has very carefully inspired Spiritualists to change the term "casting out of demons" to "rescue work"* and from time to time, mediums are specially chosen for this purpose of "rescuing." However, whatever the name given to it, the practice is the same and in order to produce this counterfeit successfully, the spirits teach that as man is responsible for the expiation of his own sins, he has to learn his lesson the hard way in the lesser spheres of the spirit world.

Spiritualists are taught that the spirit world is divided into several spheres according to the various degrees of "progress" and a spirit is relegated to whatever sphere is justifiable taking into consideration the kind of life it has lived upon earth. This means that if a man has been a renegade all his earthly life, he will pass into the lesser spheres of spirit world where he will find other spirits like himself—and they remain there possibly for centuries—until there comes to them a definite consciousness of their shortcomings, followed by a desire to evolve into something better. People who commit suicide, murderers and infidels, etc., are all consigned to the lesser spheres until they are considered suitable for promotion to a higher position in the spirit world. We are not told who does the judging of suitability, presumably it is a "natural" state of evolution!

When this consciousness of their fallen condition is awakened and a desire to progress is shown, they are given an opportunity of returning to earth again by being re-born to live a more spiritual type of life in another body. This touches on the subject of *reincarnation* which is a theory held by most Spiritualists. They believe that a person can be reincarnated over and over again until they are perfected and so highly evolved that they become full of wisdom and power. They claim that this accounts for the fact that one individual is so brilliant while another is an idiot, because the former is said to have been reincarnated more times than the latter and is no doubt an "older soul." They teach that a person who is bedridden for years is really a spirit who has chosen to come back to earth in a physical body and suffer, and this accounts for the apparent cheerfulness of the invalid. The person who is born blind and cannot be cured of blindness remains blind only because the spirit of that person chooses to suffer in that way. A still-born child is a spirit who has evolved over and over again and all is needed to attain perfection was just one more very short period in a physical body after which it becomes a spirit of the highest evolution straight away. This belief also extends to animals and insects who are gradually evolving until they become human beings and so on! *Having attained the highest evolution possible in the spirit world, one becomes a ball of light,* which seems a somewhat tame ending for so many aeons of hard work! Such, however, are the pernicious doctrines that are let loose on the people who follow this cult and Satan has carefully made extra provision for the "bad" or "evil" spirits to be taught as well.

While these bad spirits are dwelling in the lesser spheres suffering for their misdeeds until repentance overtakes them, some are able to break away and return to the earth to upset the plans of the "good" spirits. They become earthbound spirits and it is this type of evil spirit that is supposed to manifest itself in a "Rescue Circle."

Mediums chosen for this type of work are regarded as "Old Souls" who know more about the spirit world than these "fallen" spirits do themselves. These spirits do not seem to appreciate being "rescued," by the way, but presumably gratitude comes later in their evolution. Rescue mediums usually co-operate with a small band of workers (who may or may not be rescue mediums themselves) and work as a team, meeting in Home Circles which take the usual form, with or without light. Usually a dim light is effected so that sitters may be able to concentrate more easily. Prayer is made for the "high" and "evolved" spirits to watch over the Circle and guide the mediums to say and do the right thing to any evil spirit that may take control of them. All concentrate on the work, sending out thoughts to the "evil" spirits to attract them to the Circle, the idea being to allow the evil spirit to control a rescue medium, the other members of the Circle then attempt to instruct the controlling spirit as to how and why it should learn to evolve on to another sphere. Then the trouble starts! Spirits come through using the worst blasphemy imaginable, very often throwing the medium to the ground and furniture is quite often hrown at the sitters if they are not quick enough to prevent it. In well-conducted Circles of this nature, rooms are usually emptied to be on the safe side excepting for the chairs of the sitters and the medium, as "evil" spirits are liable to cause much damage to crockery, ornaments, etc., if these remain in the vicinity. Attempts have been made to murder some of the sitters or the medium himself, but an experienced team is, of course, fully aware of the methods of these "evil" spirits. The team will watch the medium very carefully and as soon as he shows signs of spirit control, he will be firmly held by two or three members of the team so that he cannot struggle. These people are gullible enough to believe that if they hold the medium in a certain way the "evil" spirit will not be able to escape and will remain fixed in the body, compelled to stay until they release it. This somewhat rough handling is considered to be in the interests of the medium's own safety as there is no knowing what the spirits may do if the team is not sufficiently alert.

The medium will show great strength during this process of being held and will attempt to struggle as much as possible. A lot depends upon the strength of the team, therefore, at this stage, and as well as exerting their physical strength, they must at the same time exert mental pressure and plead with the controlling spirit, explaining that they only want to help it and that they are really friends. Eventually they manage to pacify it. The demon makes sure that he allows the team to be successful in the course of time; it would be unwise to discourage the sitters to the point of making them give up altogether. His counterfeit plans would be thwarted if they got to this point.

Having eventually managed to calm the spirit which may have taken some considerable time, the team will speak kindly to it. At first it will pretend that it doesn't want to be spoken to at all and will refuse to hold a conversation. Nevertheless it continues to curse and swear, repeatedly saying, "Why are you tormenting me?" or "You are the children of Light coming to persecute me." The spirit will not show itself at all keen to "see the light" and if it becomes obstreperous, one of the team will allow his spirit "guide" to take control of the Circle and incidentally of himself, and the so-called "good" spirit, that is to say, the guide will talk to the "bad" spirit and reason with him. This apparently being more effective than the team dealing with it, the "bad" spirit then gives out a whole rigmarole of past misdeeds which he confesses with gusto, and seeks forgiveness from the "good" spirit and the team, which confession is met with the required forgiveness from the worn-out members of the team and they will leave the repentant spirit in the hands of the "good" spirit guide, with whom it will trot off happily to the higher spheres where it can be taught to be of service to mankind.

It may be well to explain at this stage that Spiritualists believe that the spirits are drawn into the Circle by a love ray which comes from the sitters. It does not necessarily follow that all these "bad" spirits will be obstreperous, as some of them are presumed to be merely ignorant that they are really "dead" and the love ray has attracted them to the body of the medium. This kind of spirit will express surprise when told that it is in the "wrong" body and if asked if it remembers anything just prior to this invasion of the Circle, it will probably say that the last thing it remembers is being run over or of being in great pain upon a bed. The next thing it remembers is finding itself sitting in a Circle with the people it is talking to, feeling very surprised and after explanations all around is politely sorry for having intruded, especially as it seems to have intruded not only into the Circle, but into someone else's body as well. A most embarrassing position to suddenly awake to, I should think. It is then explained to the poor spirit that there are many more highly developed spirits who are nearby, waiting and willing to help it and show it what to do. I was once dealing with a spirit of this nature, and the invading spirit asked me what it would have to do now that it had no body. When told it would have to work on the "other side" it was extremely annoyed and left in a hurry, saying that it had never done a day's work in its life and wasn't going to start now at such an age! This may sound a little far-fetched, but the "work" idea is believed by Spiritualists because it is part of the teaching of highly evolved spirits. One works harder after one is passed over, apparently, than one does down here, for the good of oneself and to help aspiring mankind in general.

The subtlety of this kind of play acting is easily seen, but somehow or other it is very convincing to one not well versed in God's laws and who does not realize that Satan himself appears as an angel of Light and can appear to cast out demons. Truly he has blinded their eyes.

Recently there was a case on similar lines to the general one discussed above, enacted in an old house in Hampstead. The occupants of the house had, some little time after having taken up residence there, been plagued by an invisible force that woke them during the night by knocks and bangings which they considered far too loud and deliberate to be accounted for by normal means. Bedclothes were taken off, furniture and books, etc., were shifted around and anything that could be filled (i.e., saucepans, vases, ash-trays, etc.) was filled with water. Finally they appealed to a medium to go and try to "lay the ghost." A small seance was held in the house and the medium immediately went into a trance, becoming possessed instantly by a spirit who flung himself (in the body of the medium) at the feet of the medium's husband present in the Circle and also himself a medium. The spirit sobbed with apparent terror and asked to be saved because he didn't know what he was doing and "they" were after him ("they" were defined later). The man answered the spirit assuring it that there was no need for fear and attempted to solicit details. The spirit claimed to be that of an old enemy of the owner of the house who had died and been in the spirit world about a year, and had continued from that exalted sphere to attempt to harm his old enemy, the houseowner, in any way possible. In following out his attempts he had automatically attracted a whole group of very unpleasant spirits who came to help him turn the house upside down and generally make it so uncomfortable for the owner and his wife that they would be driven to leave the house, thus losing a considerable amount of money as well as experiencing distress of mind and a certain amount of physical upset. Now the poor spirit, who had this pretty motive in sight at the beginning of his operations, was alarmed at the presence of his unwanted spirit helpers and begged to be saved from them! The medium's husband soothed the distraught spirit, made it apologize for the evil of its past behavior and pray for help to put it right, and the spirit then withdrew from the medium's body. Its place was taken by an African Witch Doctor. This spirit was harder to dispose of, but evenually it accepted defeat and withdrew. Thereupon followed six or seven more devils, all of which had to come through separately, admit their fault and promise amendment. After this the medium considered her work was done, the seance finished, and there were no more demonstrations of an unwanted kind in the house after that. The owners settled down presumably to a much-earned rest. It is queer how these Rescue cases, differing in detail and circumstances, have all the same essentials and follow the same procedure.

Can the Devil really cast out demons? What are these spirits which are referred to as "evil" spirits? What are these "good" spirits which show the evil ones the "Light"? How is it done? The answer is very simple. The Devil is most certainly not casting out demons, neither is his house divided, neither are those spirits which show the others the light good spirits. In fact they are all demons! Demons have to use some method of deception in their attempt to prove the counterfeit is of God and so they play a game of make-believe. Although they are literally evil spirits, one pretends to be the "good" spirit while the other proclaims his "evil"-ness. The "evil" spirit starts first, finding no difficulty in cursing and swearing and taking great care that he does not overcome the team of workers too often, occasionally pretending to be mastered by them. The act is well-planned. On the other hand the other demon is acting as a "good" spirit, professing to be highly evolved and able to deal with "bad" spirits for their own good. The so-called "good" spirit speaks to the "evil" spirit who at first appears to be antagonistic, but eventually obeys orders and they both trot off together to laugh at the credulity of human nature that makes it possible for such a hoax to be played out.

Certainly Satan has not cast out demons because

they still remain in control of the seance, but Spiritualists, blindly believing they are doing God's work, cannot see that the Devil has managed to produce a double counterfeit of the casting out of demons. *They will argue from the Scriptures that if Spiritualism is of the Devil, it would not be possible for them to cast out evil spirits.* Satan has managed to establish another lie in the heart of man, which is his ultimate aim in using such a long drawn-out farce. This rescue work achieves a very pleasing result to Satan since few people will suspect that a demon would appear to cast out another demon. Consequently many can be deceived in this direction into believing that Spiritualism must be of God. Even Spiritualists that do not believe in a personal God believe in some kind of good power, a sort of concentrated spiritual goodness, quite unknowable but which is the source of inspiration to them to perform these works. We can, however, compare the methods of these "Rescue Circles" with the Word of God, and we find that the demons in such circles are not cast out IN THE NAME OF JESUS. They are not commanded to come out, but are pleaded with and attempts are made to convince them of the error of their ways. Some Spiritualist circles may make great play of the leadership of the Lord Jesus, in the singing of hymns, etc., but His Name is not used with authoritative power as we are commanded to use it.

Our Lord cast out demons by a word of command, "come out of him . . ." So it should be with the Church today, as one of the signs following them that believe. May we as a body seek to cast out demons only in the Name of the Lord Jesus Christ, not disregarding the Spiritualists' challenge that they cast out evil spirits while the Church sleeps.

Such exhibitions of power on behalf of Satan and

his fallen angels is indeed a challenge to our faith in these latter days, and we should seek a blessed outpouring of the Spirit of God, Who has given us power as individuals to overcome by the Blood of the Lamb and the word of our testimony. In the Name of Jesus may we cast out demons. One day they will all bow the knee to our gracious Lord, but let the Church seek to be filled with the Holy Ghost now and gain a present victory, through Christ Jesus, and Him alone.

CHAPTER XI

PHYSICAL PHENOMENA

*". . . to another, faith by the same Spirit . . . to another the
working of miracles. . . ."*

I COR. 12:9-10.

THE types of mediumship we have hitherto dealt with
(with the exception of Rescue work) fall under the
category of mental mediumship. Now we approach
"physical" mediumship—a type very appealing to the
average person. Physical phenomena (which include
the use of ectoplasm, transfiguration and direct voice)
is a method used by the spirits which enables the on-
lookers to either see, hear or feel the spirits for them-
selves, regardless of their being "mediums" them-
selves. A medium is, of course, used by the spirits to
effect these results. It will be remembered that in
types of mental mediumship as we have already consid-
ered, nothing is seen or heard by the listener apart
from the actual spirit guide speaking through the me-
dium's body and using his voice while under control
or trance. It may perhaps be mentioned here that
usually when a medium is in trance and the communi-
cating guide takes control of his body, there is some-
times a slight contortion of the medium's face and
body suggestive of the character of the guide. This is
difficult to explain, but if for instance the guide was an

Ancient Egyptian, the medium's face becomes to a certain degree composed of a set expression which gives an impression of age-old learning and civilization and an amount of sternness which one would expect from such an "old" spirit. This set expression is repeated with remarkable duplication each time that particular guide comes through to speak and becomes recognizable and even familiar, as one sits in a circle regularly with that particular medium. This can be seen by any of the sitters who possess any capabilities of natural discernment, irrespective of their spiritual capacities. Also the spirit appears to impress his presence and even *stature* upon the medium, which is somehow *felt*, tangibly almost, by the sitters. Here again it is difficult to describe what is only a sensation, but granting that the controlling spirit is supposed to have been a big strong man when upon earth, and possibly the medium may be a person of small size, somehow or other as the spirit takes over the body, the sitter gets a strong impression of "largeness" as if he were sitting very near to a huge person, although the medium's body presumably does not literally expand. However, in spite of these impressions, it is still more satisfying to see, hear or handle something that is even more tangible, and physical phenomena are an attractive stage for people who like to believe "only what their eyes can see," so to speak.

During this sort of seance the operating spirits make use of a substance which is drawn from the medium's own body. This substance is a semi-luminous thick vapor which oozes from the medium's mouth, ears, nose, eyes, or from the stomach and is dimly visible in the gloom. This mist which gradually becomes solid, as it eventually makes contact with the natural surroundings of the seance room, is called *ectoplasm* and is the basis of physical phenomena.

Ectoplasm being sensitive to light, necessitates the seance being conducted in darkness. Experiments have been made to produce ectoplasm in light with, however, only limited success. Nevertheless, photographs in darkness have been taken with special cameras and they present a very strange and repulsive sight, with the ectoplasm hanging down like icicles from the mouth, nose, etc., of the medium. When touched (only permissible by the controlling guide) it will move back into the body and if suddenly seized the medium will scream out or be caused to be violently sick. Such sudden graspings of ectoplasm have very often caused great bodily harm to the medium and could even result in loss of life. The reason for this being so dangerous is that the ectoplasm becomes solid through contact with the air and before it is able to enter back into the medium's body in the normal way, it has to dematerialize to its original state. If touched suddenly, without warning or permission, or unexpectedly contacted with light, the solid ectoplasmic mass will rush straight back to the body of the medium before having a chance to dissolve to its natural state. I have known of many mediums who have been crippled or blinded for life owing to the sudden impact of the solid ectoplasm which springs back with as much force as if it were connected to the medium by an excessively strong piece of elastic. I myself was blinded for nearly 24 hours after such an incident occurred. The force of the ectoplasm against the stomach caused a scar from side to side, which took many days to disappear.

Ectoplasm can, however, be touched harmlessly with the permission of the guide and I could quote cases where permission has been granted for a piece of it to be actually cut off for a closer examination to be made. *Under scrutiny the substance appears to be like something between cheese muslin and a sheet of fine linen*—this accounts for many physical mediums being charged with fraud and convicted, for investigators have sometimes thought that it was cheese muslin provided beforehand by the medium to hoodwink the sitters. What has occasionally happened is that the suspicious investigator has grasped or attempted to grasp the ectoplasm which has rushed back to the medium's body, dragging the investigator with it, and the investigator has, possibly naturally, come to the conclusion that it was some kind of a sheet enveloping the medium and himself. The medium was then charged with fraud, and punished by law. A medium was charged in this way, comparatively recently, but strangely enough the witnesses against her were quite unable to produce the actual "sheet." The medium was sent to prison protesting her innocence and spent most of the time in the hospital. It was agreed by Spiritualists that she was a genuine medium and evidence was produced in court to justify her innocence, but the jury was not satisfied and passed sentence just the same.

Actual frauds are really very rare in the Movement and when such cases are known, Spiritualists are the first expose them. It is, however, possible to fake, but the pretender would need a great deal of experience and the possibility of exposure would be so great that impostors do not consider it unless prepared to openly admit that they are only tricksters doing such things merely for public entertainment and not professing to be Spiritualists. There have been many successful Theatre Magicians, who have been able to produce types of phenomena similar to that produced in a seance, but this does not alter the fact that something is definitely behind the strange demonstration of power and this something is just as obviously supernatural.

I have seen ectoplasm produced under severe test conditions that would render faking an impossibility. Mediums have been thoroughly searched before the seance, others, clad only in a bathing costume, have been securely bound and held by people in the seance while ectoplasm has been produced just the same. Strange things have happened in these physical seances; sometimes people have been raised from the floor without anyone touching them. It is recorded that people have floated out of a window and back through another. This is called *levitation* and has been witnessed by numerous crowds of people at various times and places, and can hardly be put down to the imagination of the minority. Another form of physical phenomena is "Telekinesis"—this is when objects are moved around the room, articles carried through walls and locked doors without being damaged in any way. Musical instruments played without anyone touching them, presents of flowers and jewelry given to sitters.

Mediums have been known to free themselves from bonds during trance conditions while others can touch red hot coals without being burnt. These miracles are performed not only in the Congo by witch doctors, but in England. Satan is producing miracles and showing many signs and wonders that are strong in deceptive power. The gifts of the working of miracles and faith are counterfeited by demons—a challenge to the true Church of Christ.

Physical phenomena serves many purposes so far as Satan is concerned and he will use his counterfeit of these two supernatural gifts to suit his own ends and in order that people may think that the operation of the counterfeit is really "divine."

Through this type of mediumship people have been miraculously saved from danger, accidents and death —one medium was grasped by spirit hands just as she was falling down a precipice and saved. Man's needs can be met by the ability of the spirits to provide food for the hungry. The dead can be raised through this type of mediumship as will be seen in the chapter dealing with materialization.

One would only have to see the counterfeit in operation to realize that the nine gifts of the Spirit are for use in the Church today. It is quite obvious to the child of God that Satan would not go to so much trouble to copy the divine gifts with such accuracy, if God had withdrawn them from the Church in these last days. Satan is able to blind the eyes of people into believing that Spiritualism is the "true religion" because they have what seem to be the gifts of the Spirit, whereas the Church is either sleeping or denying the necessity of these supernatural gifts. Surely the Church should stand four-square on the Word of God, Who commands that we be filled with the Holy Ghost. If demons are able to work such miracles through mediums, how much more would the Holy Spirit work through the true Church of believers, with mighty signs and wonders following those that believe!

As we progress further into physical mediumship we come to "Transfiguration." Although the majority of mediums have to wait a long time before they reach perfection in this direction, it is really one of the more common types of physical phenomena. Transfiguration Circles or seances are almost invariably held in the medium's own home, although there are occasional open meetings for a limited number of sitters at different Spiritualist churches. Visitors can sit either in the Circle or in rows and the medium will be seated in full view of the sitters. Prayers are offered and lights are turned out while a small spotlight is shown on to the face of the medium who will then go into trance. (The opening prayers, of course, depend on whether the sitters believe in the value of prayer or not, otherwise the proceedings carry on without it.) Although as a general rule the mediums go into trance, it does not imply that it is impossible for physical phenomena to take place without trance condition as successful results have been obtained either way.

Sitters will anxiously wait, watching the medium, and after a time a mist will be noticed which almost obliterates his face. Gradually out of the mist appears features that are entirely different from that of the medium. It can be the face of a woman, man or child. The face thus materialized will look in the direction of one of the sitters in the meeting who will then acknowledge it. Sitters who know the rules of seances or ordinary Spiritualist meetings, will not give any information to the communicating spirit in case it is not a "good" spirit, and the manifestation is desired to be as evidential as possible. They will not just call out to the spirit, "Are you such and such a person?" It will be left to give its own name and proof of identity without help or coaxing.

The remarkable thing about transfiguration is the fact that when the face of the spirit appears, the eyes take on the actual color of the dead person that the spirit states itself to be, regardless of the color of the medium's own eyes which, in any case, remain closed during the seance. Various faces will appear, one after another; some will be guides of different nationalities, speaking in different tones and languages, and messages and conversations take place. Tears are shed at the many reminders of the fact that these spirits are supposed to be loved ones who are watching over those left behind on earth. Tears of joy, tears over the fact of forgiveness expressed by these spirits towards a particular sitter who may have wronged them while on earth. This *forgiveness* is a great point on the "other side" and very consoling to somebody left on this side with a slightly guilty conscience that would no doubt follow them all the rest of their lives, apart from the contact of these spirits. Such kind words are spoken on both sides, by both spirits and sitters, and many blessings are passed from one to another, so that all seems to be of one accord with "love" thought going out towards the medium so that he may have more "power."

When the phenomenon has finished, the medium gives permission for the lights to be turned on and the sitters disperse to their homes where they are able to meditate over the "goodness" of the spirits in allowing such wonderful things to happen through earthly vessels. How many precious souls fall victim to these seducing spirits! The Devil has inspired his blinded followers to have complete faith in the spirits and because of their simple faith and trust, he obliges them with miracles and "signs" following.

Another type of mediumship is "Direct Voice" which requires darkness, but here again some attempts have been successful in ordinary light.

Direct Voice mediums are generally referred to as "Trumpet" mediums, as for this purpose a small trumpet is placed in the center of the Circle. This trumpet is painted with a luminous paint to enable it to be seen in the dark. After the lights are turned out the medium will go into trance (if he is a trance medium) and his guide will enter the body to give instructions to the sitters in case there are many newcomers ignorant of this type of phenomenon. If the medium is not a trance medium he will make it his business to explain the procedure before the seance. Part of the explanation is that the ectoplasm used for this purpose will extend from the medium's own body to the trumpet and will form a rod which is referred to as an ectoplasmic rod. It will be mentioned that the trumpet will then rise from the floor and float around the room. Eventually the voice of the spirit will be heard speaking through the trumpet. The ectoplasm will become solid around the vocal chord of the spirit who is trying to communicate in this way, thus enabling it to speak. The trumpet is for it to speak through so that it can be heard. On no account must the trumpet be touched without permission. It should be mentioned also that some direct voice mediums do not use the trumpet for this purpose but rather an ectoplasmic voice mould, but this is not a very common occurrence and most of them use the trumpet.

The sitters wait in silence, sitting with legs uncrossed and hands open to extend power towards the medium who needs all they can give. They will then be commanded to sing to stimulate vibrations, the room will become cold and the atmosphere tense. Suddenly there will be a tapping sound on the trumpet, the guide explains that spirits are approaching, and the trumpet itself will be seen to rise rapidly from the floor, floating around the seance room. It will float as high as the ceiling, far beyond the reach of anyone, past the sitters, missing them by inches, and at such an incredible speed that it is a wonder that nothing is broken. The trumpet will fly past the sitters, dodging in and out, first high, then low, far and near. One sitter

was once heard to remark that the things must have
had eyes to see where they were going in the darkness.
Truly there are eyes behind it that guide it on its path-
way, but they belong to the prince of power of this
world! After careening round the room for a few mo-
ments (the sitters still singing as volubly as they can)
the trumpet stops dead in front of one of them and a
voice speaks. The voice will say to whom it belongs
and give satisfactory evidence as to its identity and
there will follow a short conversation. After that there
will be other spirits speaking, all purporting to be dif-
ferent personalities. I remember one that stated itself
to be the spirit of the late Dame Clara Butt, singing
"Abide with Me," with such accuracy and style that
would only have been possible by that great singer
herself. It would have been *humanly* impossible to im-
itate such a unique voice except by supernatural
power, but the demons know us so intimately that
they can perfectly well imitate our voices and man-
ners.

At some of these seances mediums will use as many
as four or five trumpets at once, all flying around in
different directions without knocking against each
other, all speaking in different voices at the same time,
which does more or less prove the integrity of the me-
dium, as he could hardly be speaking in four or five
different voices simultaneously.

The seance may last for an hour or more before the
power will gradually die down. The trumpets will
move at a slower pace, getting nearer and nearer to
the floor and performing a perfect landing on the exact
spots where they stood before the commencement of
the seance. Is not this indeed a miracle? Is not this cer-
tainly supernatural? The only answer is, "Yes, it cer-
tainly is supernatural." Faking is possible, no doubt, as

in all other cases, but not in as many instances as these things occur; there would be no point in such wholesale trickery.

Some Spiritualists claim that when the Voice of God was heard at the baptism of the Lord in Jordan saying "This is my beloved Son, in Whom I am well pleased," it was by the manifestation of "Direct Voice" mediumship. Where in this case, was the trumpet? Where was the voice mould? Where was the dark room and the singing sitters to keep up vibrations.

Even though we know God's judgment on Spiritualism we have sufficient evidence of supernatural power to convince us of our need of a divine filling of the Holy Ghost. If we have not experienced this, the evidence given above should cause us to seek this filling and the gifts of the Spirit, which the Lord has promised to those that believe. We can indeed thank God that at this present time there are those of His children who stand firm upon His promises and He is confirming their faith with the signs following. No wonder the Devil desires to counterfeit the gifts to such an extent and to mislead people who might otherwise follow the true Light which comes from God alone, by Christ Jesus. Let us see to it that our whole trust is in Him, Who shall teach us to discern good from evil and the divine from the satanic.

CHAPTER XII

MATERIALIZATION

*". . . and as ye go, preach, saying The Kingdom of Heaven
is at hand . . . raise the dead. . . ."*
MATT. 10:7-8,

CONCLUDING the study of gifts of miracles and faith as
found in counterfeit in physical phenomena, we now
come to *Materialization. This is the power to raise the
presumed spirits of the dead in visible form which can
be seen by all the sitters whether they have psychic
gifts or not.*

The reader will remember that in mental medium-
ships, spirits are described by the mediums to the sit-
ters or congregation before they are able to be recog-
nized, but *in materialization this is not required as
they appear in a more or less solid and tangible form.*

This places the medium in great danger, and materi-
alization meetings are not therefore open to the pub-
lic. Entrance to these seances is limited exclusively to
those who can be trusted not to cause untoward dis-
turbances, although some do manage to enter under
false credentials. The sitters gather around in the
usual circle; the medium will either join this or sit in a
special cabinet designed for the purpose. Lights are
turned out, prayer is given if desired, and the spirit
guide takes control of the medium. It gives instruc-

tions to members of the seance, adds the usual warning against touching the ectoplasm or the spirit that will materialize without permission from the guide or manifesting spirit and the seance begins. Sitters start the ball rolling by singing lively songs to arouse vibrations, while dimly visible in the darkness will be seen the semi-luminous ectoplasm emanating from the medium. As this pours out into the center of the room it gradually builds up into a definite form. At first it appears as a column of mist, but slowly the features begin to clarify themselves. The gradual process of building holds the sitters spellbound, as they see the body forming, first the feet, then legs, body, arms and face. The complete form of the spirit will then walk around (being very careful not to walk on the feet of the sitters and to step over anything that may be in its way) until it finds the person with whom it wishes to hold a conversation. Several spirits can appear and speak at the same time and very often it is possible to produce materialization together with "direct voice" as in the previous chapter. I recall a room full of materialized forms, all speaking at the same time, while luminous trumpets were seen floating around in the darkness, avoiding sitters and materialized spirits alike, while the voices of other spirits were heard speaking through the trumpets. Sitters are expected to continue singing unless the spirit is actually speaking to them, which seems a little rude on the face of it, but apparently the singing helps them in some queer way. Naturally excitement is rife with such wonders taking place in the room, spirits walking around, trumpets in mid-air and everything extremely jolly and friendly. I once had water thrown over me by a "jolly" spirit for not singing—materialized spirit water, presumably, since there was no other water in the room to my knowledge. I can also recall shaking hands with a spirit and it would be beyond words to describe the peculiar sensation caused at the realization that one is actually holding the hand of what is supposed to be the spirit of one raised from the dead! The coldness of the touch, the hardness of the grip, and the feel of the "bones" and "knuckles" sends a chill throughout one's body. Rest assured that the majority of the sitters who are permitted to take the hand of the materialized spirit will make sure that he counts the knuckles and fingers, not being too ready to believe anything, even the evidence of his own eyes, and after having done so, there is a feeling of awe at the fact that a spirit has actually been handled. On another occasion I was permitted to cut a lock of hair from a spirit and to pat a spirit "dog" and to stroke a spirit "cat." Spirit animals are produced together with birds and other creatures in these seances as well as spirit people. This draws animal lovers naturally, especially those who have been particularly attached to pets that have gone the way of all flesh.

What is supposed to have once been a living human being now has to depend on another human frame to provide ectoplasm to enable it to materialize! Truly they seek a body in which to dwell and will go all out to dwell in something else if a human body is not available. They are glad to avail themselves of anything solid. *We hear from our missionaries of idol worshippers, how figures are created from stone and wood and the heathen worshippers call on the spirits to come in and dwell in them.* They tell us that these people worship the idols because they realize that an evil spirit has actually come to dwell in their handmade gods. *Missionaries state that the evil power is*

*definitely there, that it is not mere superstition but de-
mons really do dwell in these idols of stone and wood.*

Considering physical phenomena from the point of
view of the demons' great desire to enter into a body,
we can see the reason why ordinary control and trance
is more common than materialization, because in the
former they can have a body to dwell in, thus giving
relief. We can see why spirits encourage believers to
sit in Developing Circles to prepare for trance condi-
tions so that demons may enter in to gain this relief
even if for only a short time. It also explains why there
are not many of these physical mediums and why it
takes so long to develop such phenomena as this. I
know of a medium who was so desirous of being a
physical one that he sat with a trumpet every night for
thirteen years before he managed to produce even a lit-
tle tapping in the trumpet. Then it was another nine
years before he was able to successfully produce the
voice. The best part of a life-time, twenty-two years,
waiting for demons to oblige—yet he believed! This is,
of course, an exception to the general rule.

Spiritualists claim that materialization is the same
type of mediumship that Jesus used when He called
Lazarus from the grave, but the Scriptures tell us em-
phatically that Lazarus arose because Jesus called him
by name. There was no mention of darkness, or ecto-
plasm, neither was there a gradual building up of Laz-
arus' body, because his physical body was already
there, bound in grave clothes. When Jesus called "Laz-
arus, come forth!" it meant that only Lazarus was to
arise. The Lord knew that He had to call him by his
name; otherwise there is a strong possibility that all
the dead would have arisen at the command of the Al-
mighty God, speaking in those tones. We note that he
did not disappear again as do the spirits in seances but

remained alive and presumably lived a normal life. This was a literal raising from the dead!

Spiritualists also claim materialization to have been employed in the case of the witch of Endor (I Sam. 28). According to their viewpoint this "good woman" was a genuine medium who at the appearance of Samuel was so awestruck at his being such an important patriarch that she became afraid! No doubt this woman was a genuine medium, there is no reason to believe otherwise, but she was obviously deluded like all mediums by a familiar spirit. However, seeing that Spiritualists like to use Scriptural incidents to back up their claims, we will most certainly turn to the Word of God which is the measuring line of all doctrine. In Leviticus 20:6, we find that one who consults a person with a familiar spirit will be put to death, and in Deut. 18:10-11, we also see that it is an abomination for one to "have" a familiar spirit. This clearly means both mediums and inquirers are condemned in the Word of God. Furthermore, we find that the Hebrew word for familiar spirit is "Ohv" which in the modern language of today would be interpreted "bad spirit." No doubt at the time of the translation the word "familiar" meant "belonging to the family," thus denoting a spirit which was on intimate terms with the deceased person. It is recorded in I Sam. 28:7 that King Saul wished to consult, literally, "a woman that is mistress of, or, controls, a departed spirit." Regarding this incident of Saul and the Witch of Endor, when God allowed Samuel to return, we notice three very important things which remind us of the *sin* of *Spiritualism*:—

> (1) The medium was afraid at the appearance of Samuel.

(2) Samuel was annoyed and said, "Why hast thou disquieted me?"

(3) Saul died, not only because he had transgressed and displeased God (as Spiritualists choose to have it), but also because he consulted one that had an "Ohv." (1 Chronicles 10, 13.)

In choosing this incident to back up their claims of communication with the dead, Spiritualists condemn themselves. For the medium to be afraid, made this particular seance somewhat unusual; the fact that Samuel was annoyed at being "brought up" also shows that it was not the usual thing for spirits to be so pleased at contacting human beings as they are supposed to be these days, and Saul's death, due in part (and there is nothing to indicate that it is a small part either) to having consulted a medium, all go to show that it is not the Lord's will that communication should be established between the living and the dead, except in the one or two instances where He has had some extraordinary purpose in allowing it to happen. These rare exceptions prove the rule, and who are we to insist, as do Spiritualists, that the exceptions shall become the rule at all times. The Lord alone still has the power to kill and to make alive, and to pass His judgments as He pleases.

Another favorite example is taken from the account of the Mount of Transfiguration in Matthew 17, and they claim that this incident was an open-air seance! How strange that 2,000 years ago it was possible for a seance of this nature to be held in the open air, in full daylight, when now, with all our scientific knowledge, it still has to be performed in darkness. We can again ask where was the ectoplasm? Did the disciples have to sing lively songs, the Galilean equivalent to "Knees

up Mother Brown," and similar songs which are favor-
ites frequently heard in modern seances? Perhaps they
managed to stir up the vibrations in some other way
and thus make the materialization possible? They will
bring this transfiguration scene forward to prove their
point that the dead can return and communicate with
earth as demonstrated so perfectly in this particular
incident. Again we will turn with pleasure to the
Word of God and we find that in II Kings 2:11, that
Elijah went up by a whirlwind into heaven. Not the
usual way of entering, as he did not see death in the
normal procedure. Is this such a perfect example of
the return of people who have died a natural death?
Surely this again is an exception to the general rule, so
can hardly form a corollary. "There is still Moses to
account for," they will say, "he died all right because
the Bible says so." Quite so, Moses did die and "God
buried him" (Deut. 34:5-6). No one saw him die, but
we have to grant that he did die. "Just like Samuel,"
says the Spiritualist, "and he returned in the same
way." It is obvious that both Samuel and Moses died
and we do not dispute the fact, neither can we deny
that they returned for a specific purpose. There is an
element in the death of Moses since he was buried by
God alone and no one has yet discovered his sepulchre
with any degree of accuracy, that is beyond the ordi-
nary case, as there was an element in the passing of
Elijah, so that neither can be put forward as average
cases. There is nevertheless even taking it on face
value, a mighty difference between the return of Sam-
uel, Moses and Elijah—in the permissive will of
God—to the wholesale extent of the "return" of spirits
in modern day seances. The two incidents referred to
were very obviously great exceptions to the normal
course of events. Spiritualists would have us believe

that it is as normal for spirits to return to earth as it is for humans to eat and drink and breathe the air around them. Also, in the case of Samuel, he was allowed to return to tell Saul about his coming *death*. In the case of Moses and Elias, on the Mount of the Transfiguration, they also came to talk to Jesus of His *death*. Demons who impersonate the dead in seances try to prove the first recorded lie of the Devil by teaching that "there is *no death*" and that it is only a delusion. Satan gives himself away by going too far and becoming unable to retract. Once he starts he has to carry on with his blasphemy deluding people to believe his old lie, "Ye shall not surely die," and thereby showing them a way into a realm of knowledge that has been forbidden by God. By assuring them that there is no death, he also keeps their minds from thinking of the "second" death, which should be of even greater consideration to their eternal destiny.

This practice of Spiritualism, as it is called in the Western world, going under various names of witchcraft, demon worship and priestly superstition in the East, is bringing millions of blinded believers into darkness and ensuring their eternal damnation. Nevertheless, the Spiritualistic claim that they can raise people from the dead and their faith in the performance of these things and even their patience in waiting for the spirits to condescend to use them, bring the challenge afresh to Christians. Again we need to ask ourselves if we are fulfilling the commission which the Lord has given to us. He instructed His disciples not only to preach that the kingdom of heaven is at hand but also to raise the dead. He is as ready to honor His Word as ever He was, and our faith likewise if we are obedient to His commands. The signs following would indeed follow, as the result of our obedience and of our really touching God in prayer for the fulfilment of His living Word. He is just the same today!

CHAPTER XIII

TRYING THE SPIRITS

"Beloved, believe not every spirit, but try the spirits and see whether they are of God; because many false prophets are gone out into the world. . . ."
I JOHN 4:1.

"To the law and to the testimony; if they speak not according to this word, it is because there is no light in them. . . ."
ISAIAH 8:20.

IT must be obvious to the unbiased reader of the previous chapters that a cult that can claim so many earnest adherents as Spiritualism does at this present day must have a definite reality about it, and is very far from being all imagination or the results of clever hoodwinking by mediums of credulous people. Obviously again this Movement—as do all Movements—must suffer to some degree from over-credulous people that make it easy for deliberate deception to take place, but *one cannot judge a whole Movement by a small minority of individuals.* However, allowing for this gullibility, it is still a matter of strong inference that *something* really does happen at seances that can and does convince sane and intelligent people that spirit communication is not only possible but can become an everyday experience and that these communications do develop to earnest seekers into a system of teaching, which is bound to some extent to alter their outlook on life. *Since this cannot be denied the only question that remains is not its reality but its origin.* Spiritualists claim that they have contact with spirit "guides" and the spirits of people who have died or departed from the earth. The Scriptures are equally definite in stating that man has no contact with departed spirits or they with us, e.g., Job 14:21; Eccl. 9:5; also Luke 16:26. Neither are "spirit guides" offered to the Christian—"There is one God and one Mediator between God and men, the Man Christ Jesus . . ." (I Tim. 2:5) *Anybody else acting as a "go-between between God and man would not only be superfluous but blasphemous* . . . "He that believeth not God hath made Him a liar, because he believeth not the record that God gave of His Son" (I John 5:10).

Seeing then that the Bible is so clearly against all contact with the departed, how do we account for the phenomena that takes place in modern Spiritualistic seances? Men like Sir Oliver Lodge and Sir Arthur Conan Doyle were both men of renown and there is no reason to doubt that their statements are true, as far as facts are concerned. Their conclusions drawn from these facts are another matter. We must grant that phenomena does take place and we can therefore come to but two conclusions, either of which the reader must decide for himself as to correctness.

(1) Either God now permits that which He once forbade and condemned, or
(2) The evil spirits are at the root of all the messages received and that contact is not made with the departed dead, but with demons impersonating them.

We will deal with these separately and consider what

form these messages would take if communication with the dead was sanctioned by God. In the first instance these messages would have to be in complete harmony with the Scriptures and the Lord Jesus Christ would be exalted far above all else. We will see upon examination that the messages received are not so and many Spiritualists will openly admit the fact. To any Christian that believes that God has revealed Himself through Christ and has spoken in these last days through His Son, and that the Scriptures are indeed the Word of God and the Word of Life to them that trust in Him, *the deviation from Scripture and the complete opposition to it in many cases is sufficient to condemn the practice.*

Dealing with the second conclusion that the communicating spirits must be *"evil spirits" impersonating spirits of the dead*—what sort of messages would the listener at the seance expect to receive? *What methods would these spirits use? Naturally they would be of comfort and consolation to overcome any anxiety or worry to those left behind.* With all fear of the future gone, and death explained only as a natural process of evolution with no judgment seat at the other side of it, there is no need to take heed of the Word of God when it warns us that it is appointed unto man once to die and after death the judgment. If we believe this then we must make some definite decision and take our stand in this life, for Christ—but if we can do away with this belief for the time being, it will be too late after death to seek the grace and salvation of God, and Satan has grasped another soul to accompany him to the fire prepared for him and his angels. To accomplish this purpose the spirits will tell the listener that their loved ones are perfectly happy on the other side of life, that care and suffering are non-existent, and all this in spite of the beliefs they held—or did not hold—in this life with regard to Almighty God and the salvation He has provided for us. True, as mentioned in previous chapters, they say that if one has lived a very bad life on earth, retribution has to be made on the other side, but eventually one and all attain to perfectness, even if it takes aeons to bring this about.

In order to remove all doubt from the mind of the enquirer the evil spirit would then show some intimate knowledge of the one it is impersonating—the listener is by this time convinced that the spirit which is communicating is really and truly the spirit of a loved one. This kind of knowledge is perfectly easy for a demon to get hold of and to use. Note that up to now the evil spirit has very kindly removed all worry and anxiety, given confidence to the listener, and removed all doubts in the mind. Having accomplished this it is only to be expected that the demon will then discuss religion and Christianity which, of course, he does most efficiently. It must be remembered that the Devil knows the Scriptures better than we do, and it requires no effort on his part to quote the Bible with a subtle twist making many a child of God to stumble.

In spite of the fact that Spiritualists often quote Scriptures as a basis for their doctrines or arguments (in favour of their own viewpoint, of course) *it is to be noted that these quotations are only fragments of the Scriptures* and they do not take into consideration the sound doctrines that arise from a study of the *whole* Word of God, rightly divided. This was a sound principle in the Early Church, as Augustine taught, "Not what one Scripture says, but what *all* say." Most of the peculiar heresies of various religious sects arise from this practice of isolating texts from the whole setting, and it is to be remembered that Satan himself used the written Scriptures in an attempt to confound the Lord Himself during the temptation in the wilderness (Matt. 4:6). The use of Scriptures, therefore, is in no way a hallmark of the inspiration of God behind a Movement, although many people are led on by this apparent evidence of a heavenly benediction, even to the extent of being able to say that they have done many wonderful works in His Name (See Matt. 7:21-23). Their surprise will no doubt be as terrible as it is unexpected to receive the command, "Depart from Me, I never knew you."

The teaching of these spirits would be so full of enlightenment, of deep truths, of superior knowledge and religious matter, plus worldly wisdom, that the unconscious victim would be gradually led on into darkness without noticing that he was being surrounded by false teaching and deception, until the Bible and its teachings would be, to all practical intent, forgotten and superseded by something professing to be "deeper." Such is the method which we would expect the Devil and his emissaries to use, and that is exactly what happens!

Sir Arthur Conan Doyle, in his book *The New Revelation*, describes how he became a Spiritualist; he describes conversations with spirits, also the messages received, and states that these messages are from spirits of the departed. He also states that these spirits testify that the information given is at the Divine Will of God and that the Lord has permitted this NEW REVELATION" to be given. Presumably the revelation of Calvary is not sufficient for this modern age—we need an additional revelation to inspire us that the apostles and martyrs did not have!

On close examination of different conversations

with these so-called departed spirits, recorded at various times, we find that the methods used are exactly on the lines suggested above, that they do in fact use the very system that would be expected of evil spirits impersonating the dead, with the air and purpose of leading people away from the truth which is found in Christ. Let us look at an instance or two:—

> A spirit claiming to be a Dorothy Postlethwaite has manifested; she was a Roman Catholic, but this makes no difference in the spirit world. She states that she is in the company of Protestants, Buddhists and Mohammedans, and that she is quite happy.

One wonders what the Pope would have to say to this!

> A spirit claiming to be a well-known ·cricketer, who while on earth was a free-thinker, finds that that makes no difference either—he has not even had to suffer for the opinions held.

> A supposed son, killed in the war, appeared to his father at a seance and spoke of the good quality of the whisky and cigars supplied in the spirit world!

Surely a spirit returning from the Celestial City would have something a little more important to tell his father than those mundane things.

Satan obviously aims at making us believe that everything is happy in the after life and such information as obtained from the well-known cricketer and others is a great comfort to a bereaved parent whose son has lived a life void of God, indifferent to the claims of Christ. Such a parent would rejoice to know that in spite of the son's Godless, Christ-less life, he is still perfectly happy in the spirit world. The fear of retribution of an eternal nature has passed away from that particular enquirer who, once convinced of the genuineness of the communicating spirit, leaves himself open to believe anything that is put forward, and Satan has well prepared the ground for lying deceptions that will in the course of time lead the victim completely away from Christ.

Sir Arthur Conan Doyle admits in his *New Revelation* that Spiritualism is contrary to the Bible, yet Spiritualists will quote Scripture to back up their claims. He even says, "Though *The New Revelation* may seem destructive to those who hold Christian dogmas with extreme rigidity, it has quite the opposite effect upon the mind which has come to look upon the whole Christian scheme as a huge delusion." In other words, he considers Christianity to be a delusion to some people, admits that Spiritualism is destructive to Christianity and that those who are deluded by Christian beliefs would find Spiritualism to be "reconstructive." He evidently supposed that it is possible for those who are born again, who are blood-washed, who stand among the redeemed, to find that their whole experience has become a delusion. He little knew the power of God to make new creatures out of those who trust in Him.

Further on, in his same book, he writes, "Spiritualism would greatly modify conventional Christianity in the direction of explanation and development." It will be remembered that the serpent beguiled Eve in the same way, e.g., he pretended that he could modify God's instructions to Adam and Eve when He said, "but of the tree of the knowledge of good and evil, thou shalt not eat of it, for in the day that thou eatest thereof thou shalt surely die" (Gen. 2:17). The attitude of the serpent was one of modification, explanation and development (using the words of Sir Arthur). He modified God's instructions, explained them according to his own interpretation and developed them to suit his own ends. "Hath God said ye shall not eat of every tree of the garden?" The woman having agreed that this was so, that God had said ". . . lest ye die" (Gen. 3:3) the serpent then proceeds to modify, ye shall not surely die; for God doth know that in the day ye eat thereof, then your eyes shall be opened, and ye shall be as gods, knowing good from evil" (Gen. 3:5). Satan modified, explained and developed God's instructions and as a result of giving heed to his seductions, Adam and Eve were cast out of the garden.

The Christian can indeed rejoice in the fact that although Satan gained an apparent victory in the garden, eastward in Eden, the real victory was gained by our Saviour in the other garden of Gethsemane, where He sweat great drops of blood for us. The victory of the Cross was also gained by the Lord Jesus Christ, not by Satan, and the glorious resurrection occurred in a garden. Apparent defeat is always turned to glorious victory by our all-conquering Lord.

God Himself said that the head of Satan would be bruised and the child of God can look ahead to final victory through the blood of the Lord Jesus Christ.

Nevertheless, God is saying today, in effect, ". . . Ye shall not touch this tree (Spiritualism), ye may not eat of it, lest ye die." Satan says, "In the day ye eat of it your eyes will be opened to a new and wider revelation—ye shall surely *not* die." Modifications, explanations and developments of Christianity—a new revelation. Destructive methods are used by Satan and his hosts of demons.

Here is another statement:—

"The Christ Spirit dwells in a place above the ordinary spirit world, but far beyond that is the sphere inhabited by God, Who is so infinite as to be beyond our ken."

Here we see two deliberate statements in utter contradiction to the Word of God concerning the Lord Jesus Christ.

(1) That He is still only a spirit inhabiting His own sphere in the spirit world.

(2) That He is inferior to God the Father.

The Scriptures make it perfectly clear that He is now risen in His glorious body and is now at the right hand of God the Father. They expect us to believe that Jesus is only in the sixth sphere, while another writer tells us, in describing a seance, that a spirit manifest that claimed to be the spirit of a man who had been an infidel on earth, but who was now inhabiting the seventh sphere, one higher than the Lord Jesus Christ, Who was of spotless purity and only did the Will of the Father! From this it is to be imagined that an infidel is now inhabiting a place nearer to God than His own beloved Son in Whom He was well pleased!

Again, Sir A. Conan Doyle denies the fall of man, saying, "Man has developed from a man-like ape to ape-like man," thus indirectly backing up the Darwin theory of evolution and openly claiming that the Word of God is wrong when it says that God made man in His own image.

Sir Conan Doyle was an eminent Spiritualist in his life-time and his "spirit" still presides over one of the Spiritualist organizations (already mentioned in a previous chapter). His book is almost a text-book to Spiritualists generally speaking, so that we have a fairly high authority of general opinion in his writings.

In another Spiritualist book, entitled *Whatever is, is*

Right, we read in question and answer form "What is evil?" The reply is "Evil is good." Ques.: "What is a lie?" Ans.: "A lie holds a lawful place in creation, it is a necessity." Ques.: "What are evil spirits?" Ans.: "There is no Devil, there is no Christ."

Another Spiritualist journal describes God (as revealed in Scriptures) as harsh, cruel, vindictive and partial, going on to say, "Reasoning will soon convince that neither the personal Jesus nor the Apostles ever existed." There seems to be something queerly antagonistic to historical records here, but that apparently is of no matter to the peculiar style of reasoning expected from one.

To anyone who would ask why these spirits deny the fall of man, the reason is very clear. *If there is no fall of man, there is no need for redemption or atonement,* or *the victory of the cross* (the Lord's death becomes as ordinary as any other death) *or necessity of any power in the Blood of Christ, whereas according to scriptures, "without the shedding of blood there is no remission of sins."* Spiritualists hold the belief that man becomes his own saviour which is flat against all Scriptural teaching, e.g., Eph. 2:8-9, "For by grace are ye saved, through faith, and that *not of yourselves,* it is the gift of God, *not of works,* lest any man should boast." (See also Titus 3:5 and Acts 4:.2.)

We therefore see that Spiritualism can be nothing but communion with demons—against Scripture—and we must remember that God passed the death sentence on all mediums that had familiar spirits and also upon people consulting with them. It is sternly forbidden by God as defiling. It certainly is no new thing, but a backward movement to the worst form of heathenism and not an advance as so many Spiritualists claim. We also find in the story of Dives and Lazarus, that the Scriptures are very definite against the dead returning to earth. We see Lazarus, representing the dead in Christ, in "Abraham's bosom"—a favorite term amongst the Jews, meaning Paradise—while Dives is in Hell. Lifting up his eyes he beholds Lazarus and cries to Abraham, "Send Lazarus." It is clearly not possible for one in paradise to reach one in hell or vice-versa, as there is a gulf fixed between the two. Dives, realizing the hopelessness of his own position, cries, "Send Lazarus to warn my brethren," and again Jesus makes it plain that even if it were possible, it would serve no useful purpose because "if they believe not Moses and the prophets, they will not be persuaded by one returning from the dead," proving that it is not God's will to make contact with the dead. A gulf is set between Paradise and hell, and it is not permitted for a saint in Paradise to return to earth, but Spiritualists will claim that there is nothing to prevent Dives himself from returning to his relations as the Scriptures do not say that there is any gulf fixed between hell and earth. We know, however, that thousands of souls are passing into a Christless eternity and that the gates of hell only open inwards and not outwards; but there is no reason why Satan's fallen angels should not be able to visit the earth. They are the principalities and powers of the air and not yet confined to eternal damnation in the lake of fire.

Sir A. C. Doyle again says, "No common sense man can see any justice in vicarious sacrifice . . . too much attention has been given to the death of Christ." In other words, the death of Christ is of no more avail than that of thousands of others who have given their lives for some just cause. This is most certainly the doctrine of seducing spirits and demons.

Satan having convinced his followers that there is no fall and therefore no need of redemption, and that it is possible to amass evidence of contact with the dead, goes further with his pernicious doctrine and teaches that there is *no punishment (eternal) for sin*, nor a hell from which to be saved. At the most one only stays in the lower spheres for a matter of time, however lowly evolved one might be. All of which, of course, makes Spiritualism to be a very comfortable religion that required no heart-searching conviction of sin, and a realization of utter worthlessness before God, to establish it. The denial of these fundamental truths present Spiritualism to us with its mask off and we are able to see clearly that it is of the Devil, that the outcome of it is just what we would expect of evil spirits impersonating the departed. The Word of God is gradually torn to shreds before the eyes of believers in this cult, and the very foundations upon which the Christian faith is based are undermined. In spite of pretentions towards calling themselves "Christian Spiritualists" as so many of them do, they are in reality at the mercy of the hosts of darkness, without *the weapons which God has ordained to be used against this Enemy of our souls—the word of God which is the sword of the Spirit—and the power of the saving blood of Jesus Christ.*

We can certainly try these spirits and see whether they are of God and having done so, we find that Spiritualism is one of the most fiendish of Satan's methods of instilling lying deceptions into the minds of people. Having tested the spirits and the claims they make through their mediums, we most certainly find them contrary to the Word of God, which tells us most explicitly that "in the latter times, some shall depart from the faith, giving heed to seducing spirits and doctrines of devils" (I Tim. 4:1).

"*If they speak not according to this Word, it is because there is no light in them.*"